ON EDUCATION

ON EDUCATION

A Philosophical Dialogue

Nicholas J. Pappas

Algora Publishing
New York

Library of Congress Cataloging-in-Publication Data —

Names: Pappas, Nicholas J., author.
Title: On education : a philosophical dialogue / Nicholas J. Pappas.
Description: New York : Algora Publishing, 2018.
Identifiers: LCCN 2018043251 (print) | LCCN 2018052542 (ebook) | ISBN
    9781628943689 (pdf) | ISBN 9781628943665 (soft cover : alk. paper) | ISBN
    9781628943672 (hard cover : alk. paper)
Subjects: LCSH: Education—Philosophy.
Classification: LCC LB14.7 (ebook) | LCC LB14.7 .P355 2018 (print) | DDC
    370.1—dc23
LC record available at https://lccn.loc.gov/2018043251

Printed in the United States

TABLE OF CONTENTS

Introduction   1
1. The Point (Professor)   3
2. Environment (Musician)   5
3. Authority (Professor)   6
4. The Universe (Musician)   9
5. Selection (Professor)   12
6. Taken (Musician)   14
7. Home (Professor)   16
8. Role Models (Professor)   19
9. Roles (Musician)   20
10. Critical Thinking (Professor)   22
11. Freedom (Musician)   25
12. Culture (Professor)   27
13. Manners (Professor)   29
14. Interests (Professor)   31
15. Interests 2 (Musician)   33
16. Dreams (Musician)   36
17. Dreams 2 (Professor)   39
18. Advantage (Musician)   41
19. Civility and Respect (Professor)   43
20. Pleasure (Professor)   46
21. Pleasure 2 (Musician)   48
22. The Cause (Professor)   51

23. Drive (Musician)   53
24. Extroverts and Introverts (Professor)   54
25. Introverts and Extroverts (Musician)   57
26. Perfection (Professor)   61
27. Good Enough (Musician)   63
28. Meaning (Professor)   66
29. Meaning 2 (Musician)   69
30. Results (Professor)   71
31. Pure Science (Professor)   73
32. Patience (Professor)   76
33. Perspective (Musician)   78
34. Philosophy (Musician)   81
35. Seeds (Professor)   83
36. Conditions (Musician)   86
37. Hopes (Professor)   88
38. Common Ground (Musician)   90
39. Hierarchy (Professor)   92
40. Progress (Professor)   94
41. Literacy (Musician)   96
42. Languages (Professor)   100
43. Mother Tongue (Professor)   101
44. Wisdom (Musician)   104
45. Health (Musician)   106
46. Over-Education (Professor)   108
47. The Streets (Musician)   111
48. Fortresses (Professor)   113
49. High and Low (Musician)   114
50. Ideas (Musician)   116
51. Qualifications (Professor)   118
52. Friends (Professor)   120
53. Love (Musician)   123
54. Religion (Professor)   125
55. Power (Professor)   128
56. Meaning 3 (Professor)   130
57. Aptitude (Musician)   133
58. Resistance (Musician)   135
59. Resistance 2 (Professor)   137
60. Ease (Professor)   139
61. Fairness (Professor)   141
62. Boredom (Musician)   144

63. Analysis (Musician) — 146
64. Argument (Professor) — 147
65. Docility (Professor) — 149
66. Fragility (Professor) — 151
67. Passion (Musician) — 152
68. Culture 2 (Musician) — 154
69. Home 2 (Musician) — 156
70. Away (Professor) — 158
71. Forgetting (Musician) — 159
72. Literature (Professor) — 161
73. Math (Musician) — 163
74. Method (Professor) — 166
75. Self-Education (Musician) — 169
76. Competition (Professor) — 171
77. Machines (Musician) — 173
78. Information (Professor) — 176
79. Animals (Musician) — 177
80. Responsibility (Professor) — 179
81. Risk and Reward (Professor) — 181
82. Tastes (Musician) — 182
83. Friends 2 (Musician) — 184
84. Love 2 (Professor) — 186
85. Machines 2 (Professor) — 188
86. Necessary (Professor) — 190
87. Elites (Musician) — 193
88. Enlightenment (Musician) — 195
89. Success (Professor) — 197
90. Happiness (Professor) — 199

Introduction

Americans believe in education. Education allows you to make something of yourself. Education plays a special role in that it simultaneously provides a way out and a way in. But a way out of what? And a way into what? That's not always clear. People do expect knowledge, understanding, and maturity of those who receive education. Unfortunately, things don't always pan out. Sometimes 'education' produces a kind of learned ignorance; sometimes cliquishness; and sometimes blindness. So how do you get the good and avoid the bad?

If my aim is true, Director, a philosopher figure in this book and the others I have written, gets at the question with his two interlocutors, Musician and Professor. Musician studies with Professor. The reasons for including a professor in this book should be obvious enough. But why a musician in particular? Why not a generic student? Music is often a great passion of young people. According to some of the more influential ancient Greeks, music educates the soul. And I think this is something people today can appreciate. Music speaks to the soul; education would like to speak to the soul. Music, in the broadest sense, can be, and often is, its tool.

What is this broadest sense? And how is music a tool? The youths in question here do not like to think of music as a tool for education, or any other thing for that matter. Music liberates. Music frees. Music is beyond all other concerns. But is it? That's why the second character in this book is a musician and not someone who is concerned with engineering, for instance. Engineering is important, a necessity in our world—but who would argue it gives wing to the soul?

And here is a confession. I have long been involved with music, from an early age. I've played in bands; I make music on my computer. So there is something very personal at stake in all this for yours truly, too. In writing

I learn more than teach. That's one of the reasons I write dialogues and not treatises. I don't have a theory I'm trying to promote. I like to think someone can learn from what I've learned and still find their own way. With even the best education we must, in the end, educate ourselves. Education can point to a door, but we must walk up, turn the knob, and walk in on our own. There's no guarantee for what's behind that door. So true education takes a fair amount of courage. I'm not of the opinion that courage can be taught. We can emulate the courageous, but it's all on us.

So what am I saying? You have to be brave to read my book? What (sane) author makes that claim? It might be better to ask: who am I writing for? The answer is simple: those who've wondered about education; those who question and doubt. And my hope? That the reader will smile, perhaps be puzzled at times, but for the most part? I hope the reader enjoys.

—— Nick Pappas

Characters
  Director
  Professor
  Musician

1. THE POINT (PROFESSOR)

Director: Professor, you teach language. What's the point in that?

Professor: The point? Ha!

Director: You laugh.

Professor: Of course I laugh! But I'll answer anyway. The point is to develop an appreciation for the beauty of words.

Director: How?

Professor: My students and I study lovely old books.

Director: Why not lovely new books?

Professor: I leave the students to study those on their own.

Director: Old books require a guide?

Professor: A guide certainly helps.

Director: And you're a qualified guide because you studied with guides?

Professor: I studied with them. But I did more.

Director: What more?

Professor: I went beyond what they showed me. I taught myself all the old ways.

Director: The ways?

Professor: The ways to approach the books.

Director: And now you teach these ways to your students?

Professor: No, I teach them new ways.

Director: Why not the old ways?

Professor: Honestly? I'm tired of them.

Director: But would your students be?

Professor: No, most of them have never been exposed.

Director: Then why not expose them?

Professor: Because what's new to both is best.

Director: Both you and the students.

Professor: Yes.

Director: Why? Because it's more interesting for you?

Professor: Don't you think my students are better served when I'm more interested in what we say in class?

Director: Because you enjoy it more? And if you do, so do they?

Professor: Precisely.

Director: Then is that the goal of education? Enjoyment, both yours and theirs? I thought learning was the end.

Professor: What better to learn than how to enjoy?

Director: Some people think learning to earn is better.

Professor: Ha, ha. What's the saying? 'The more you learn, the more you earn'? That's fine — so long as you enjoy learning to earn.

Director: And if not?

Professor: I'd say you really don't want to earn.

Director: Or you're not really learning how.

Professor: True, education fails us at times.

Director: When it does, where can we turn?

Professor: To experience.

Director: Can that suffice?

Professor: You're asking if we can do without formal education? That's a big question.

Director: Yes, but isn't there an advantage in learning from life?

Professor: What advantage?

Director: We see things on our own.

Professor: Yes, but good teachers can help make things clear more quickly.

Director: What's the most important thing a teacher can help make clear?

Professor: The lesson all experience wants to teach.

Director: Which is?

Professor: How to enjoy your life.

2. ENVIRONMENT (MUSICIAN)

Musician: Many schools are like hives. They turn out perfect little worker bees.

Director: And you don't want to be perfect? Or is it that you don't want to work?

Musician: Ha, ha. You know I want to work. I want to work at my music.

Director: And can your school make you perfect at that?

Musician: I'm not looking for perfection. I'm looking to get better. And I'm looking to get better at something in particular.

Director: What?

Musician: My lyrics. So I'm studying language with Professor.

Director: Has he made you his busy little bee?

Musician: Hardly.

Director: Why not? Musicians and poets don't belong in the hive?

Musician: Some of them do. But not me.

Director: What sets you apart?

Musician: I'm not taking courses in hopes of getting good grades.

Director: Then you're a disappointment to the school.

Musician: Ha, ha. However that may be, I think Professor secretly likes it.

Director: Why do you think that is?

Musician: Because he can see I'm truly here to learn.

Director: And what you learn, you make use of right away?

Musician: That very day.

Director: That's encouraging. But tell me. I often hear musicians say they and their music are one. Is that how it is for you? And does it hold for lyrics, too?

Musician: That is how it is, and yes it does.

Director: Then I wonder if you can help me understand something.

Musician: I'll try my best.

Director: Would you say you produce music?

Musician: Sure, though I'm not strictly speaking a producer.

Director: But music is your product?

Musician: Yes.

Director: If you're one with your music, your product — does that make you a product, too?

Musician: Ha, ha. I suppose it does. But I'm my own product.

Director: Does that make you independent?

Musician: What else would?

Director: I don't know. But have you ever heard the saying that we're all products of our environment?

Musician: I have.

Director: Is there truth in that saying?

Musician: Yes, there is.

Director: Is your college part of your environment?

Musician: I suppose.

Director: Then I don't envy you.

Musician: Why not?

Director: Because of the terrible struggle.

Musician: What terrible struggle?

Director: Why, between you and your school — for what you'll turn out to be.

3. AUTHORITY (PROFESSOR)

Director: Do you ever help your students choose a profession?

Professor: If they're looking for advice? Sure.

Director: What can you be with a degree in language?

Professor: Anything you want.

Director: Oh, come on.

Professor: No, seriously. Don't we use language in everything we do?

Director: Yes, but who especially uses language? As a profession.

Professor: Teachers of language.

Director: Who else?

Professor: Writers.

Director: And?

Professor: Lawyers, to name some of the more obvious ones.

Director: Which of these three use language with authority?

Professor: They all do.

Director: Which of these three have authority themselves?

Professor: If you use something with authority, you have authority, Director.

Director: How do you teach your students this?

Professor: I teach them to be certain they know what they're talking about.

Director: Knowledge brings authority?

Professor: Of course it does.

Director: Then how do you teach students to be certain they know?

Professor: I teach them to always check their facts before they speak.

Director: And if they don't?

Professor: I catch them up when they err.

Director: How do they react?

Professor: Some get embarrassed. Others take it in stride. But there are those who resent.

Director: And what do they do? Drop out of class?

Professor: Some do. And some stew in anger for the remainder of the semester, looking for a chance to throw me.

Director: That doesn't leave them in a learning frame of mind.

Professor: No, it doesn't.

Director: So what can you do?

Professor: Offer them a chance to save face.

Director: Save face from not having known?

Professor: No, save face from allowing resentment to win.

Director: Are they sometimes too proud to accept this offer?

Professor: They sometimes don't accept. But pride isn't the problem.

Director: What is?

Professor: Their rebellion against their interests.

Director: What does that mean?

Professor: Have you ever met someone with authority who hasn't got face?

Director: Are we talking about true authority, or just a position of authority?

Professor: True authority.

Director: True authority always has face.

Professor: Well, what do these students who resent desire most?

Director: Authority?

Professor: Yes, and so when they elect not to save face when they can, this amounts to rebellion against their interests.

Director: Hmm. But what if authority isn't in their interest?

Professor: Director, isn't knowledge in all of our interest?

Director: It's hard to argue against knowing.

Professor: Yes, and we said knowledge brings authority. Were we wrong?

Director: No. Unless....

Professor: Unless what?

Director: Think of that creation story. You know, the one with the snake.

Professor: What about it?

Director: When the first ones ate of the tree of knowledge, they felt shame.

Professor: What do you think that means?

Director: They had no face even though they had knowledge. So they lacked authority.

Professor: So knowledge doesn't necessarily bring authority? I think that's the one exceptional case.

Director: Oh, I don't know. I think there are more exceptions than you might think. But let's be clear. Was eating the fruit the original rebellion against interest?

Professor: You're suggesting it was in their interest not to know? I feel like we're twisting things out of shape. The fact is, knowledge is good.

Director: And if good, it brings no shame?

Professor: None.

Director: And if no shame?

Professor: Then shameless authority holds sway. Ha, ha.

Director: Do you teach your students to have no shame?

Professor: I teach them to do nothing of which they could be ashamed.

Director: Which, as far as you're concerned, amounts to not knowing what they're talking about.

Professor: Yes. I teach them to hold their tongue, on the one hand. And I encourage them to speak, on the other.

Director: What if they don't speak when they know?

Professor: Then they should be ashamed.

Director: Why?

Professor: Because those who know have a responsibility.

Director: A responsibility to share what they know? With just anyone?

Professor: Of course not with just anyone. With those who show respect.

Director: Respect? For knowledge?

Professor: And for those who know.

4. The Universe (Musician)

Musician: I always laugh when I hear the word 'university'.

Director: Why?

Musician: It implies that the school contains the whole universe of knowledge.

Director: And it doesn't?

Musician: Ha! You know it doesn't.

Director: Where is the knowledge the university doesn't contain?

Musician: It's out there.

Director: And with a sweep of the hand you show that it's everywhere, everywhere but here.

Musician: Ha, ha! And it's true!

Director: Then why are you here and not there?

Musician: I've been there. And I'm going back.

Director: And when you're back, you'll write about what you see?

Musician: Of course.

Director: And who will listen to your music and verse? The people out there?

Musician: They will.

Director: But why?

Musician: What are you talking about?

Director: Why hear about something they already know? They do know the 'there', don't they?

Musician: Of course they do. But why will they listen? Because we love to hear what we know put to music!

Director: But what if someone doesn't know the there? Can they still love to hear?

Musician: Yes.

Director: How is that possible?

Musician: The words don't have to describe the familiar in order for us to enjoy the tune.

Director: So music can have a more or less universal appeal?

Musician: You know it can.

Director: Then the people from here, the university, might love to hear your out-there songs?

Musician: Many of them will.

Director: Why not all?

Musician: Because some are snobs.

Director: Or they simply have different tastes. Why not try to reach them?

Musician: I want to reach the people, not some narrow set.

Director: But you could appeal to this set if you wanted?

Musician: Of course.

Director: What if appealing to their tastes paid you more?

Musician: More than a hit song? I doubt it.

Director: But what if you had a guaranteed salary? Wouldn't that give you more stability to write and perform?

Musician: What salary? Are you talking about teaching?

Director: Yes.

Musician: Are you serious?

Director: Why wouldn't I be?

Musician: Do you think my fans will abandon me?

Director: No, I think just the opposite. I simply wonder what greater success will bring.

Musician: So you see the university as a sort of shelter from success? What do you think success will do to me?

Director: It will amplify your personality, good traits and bad.

Musician: And you worry about the bad.

Director: Of course. Don't you?

Musician: So what would you have me do?

Director: If you won't teach, then use the university now.

Musician: How?

Director: As a laboratory in which to explore your personality.

Musician: Know my personality for what it is and improve it where I can?

Director: Why not?

Musician: And who will I explore it with?

Director: Well, you want to know both good and bad?

Musician: I do.

Director: Then explore your personality with both those who bring out the good and those who bring out the bad.

Musician: Bring out my bad on purpose?

Director: Only for a brief time, so you can study it, yes. Or do you know another way?

Musician: I don't. Do you?

Director: Well....

Musician: What?

Director: You might study with me.

Musician: Ha! You're not part of the university.

Director: Nor do I contain the whole universe of knowledge. But I can be helpful in at least one way.

Musician: What way?

Director: I've already seen both your good and your bad.

5. SELECTION (PROFESSOR)

Director: How do you select those who'll attend your school?

Professor: We're looking for something special.

Director: Special like a gift for language?

Professor: Very much so, among other things.

Director: But for you, language is what counts.

Professor: No doubt.

Director: How can you tell a student has a gift for language?

Professor: There are a number of ways. First, they must have excellent grades in language related classes.

Director: But you can have a gift for language and not have excellent grades.

Professor: True. But we're looking for good candidates for the university.

Director: And they need good grades.

Professor: We have to show we select students based on merit.

Director: What other merit is there besides good grades?

Professor: High scores on standardized tests. Stellar references. Award-winning independent writing.

Director: But what about raw talent itself?

Professor: Talent is cheap. Refinement matters.

Director: But isn't it the job of your school to refine the talent?

Professor: Yes, but the student has to be prepared.

Director: How do you know if someone is prepared? Through grades and so on?

Professor: Those things show a willingness. And they're fairly good predictors of success. Although....

Director: What?

Professor: Sometimes people who look great on paper get here and fail out of every class.

Director: Why does that happen?

Professor: I suspect it's because they found freedom for the first time.

Director: Freedom makes you fail?

Professor: No! Lack of preparation for freedom makes you fail.

Director: What prepares you for freedom other than freedom?

Professor: Nothing. So high schools can help by giving students a taste.

Director: And then another taste, and then another? Until they've built up a sort of tolerance?

Professor: Oh, you're being ridiculous. We're not talking about building up a tolerance. We're talking about knowing how to handle yourself when you're free.

Director: And you need to know this before you arrive?

Professor: You need to know some basics. But there's much to learn when you're here.

Director: Like what?

Professor: It's impossible to say in so many words. But think of it like this. You're coming from a swimming pool and now you're plunged in the sea.

Director: But don't some students just sun themselves on the beach?

Professor: Sure. And that seems enough for them. But it's not enough if they study with me.

Director: What would you have your students do?

Professor: Dive, and hunt for pearls in the depths.

Director: Pearls of wisdom?

Professor: What else?

Director: And what good will these pearls do?

Professor: What good? Ha! You don't think wisdom is good?

Director: Not if you wear it like jewelry around your neck.

Professor: Yes, yes. But that's why you integrate this wisdom into a whole.

Director: Your whole?

Professor: Right. You make yourself whole through the words of the wise.

Director: Really? And do you promise this to your students? That they'll become whole this way?

Professor: With the best of them? I don't have to.

Director: Why not?

Professor: Because they promise that to themselves.

6. Taken (Musician)

Musician: I want to be the me I'm meant to be.

Director: Is that what everyone wants?

Musician: Of course.

Director: But how do you know what your me is meant to be?

Musician: You learn as much as you can from others, then you go off on your own and figure it out.

Director: When should you begin this process?

Musician: It starts at home.

Director: So you learn as much as you can from your family, then you go off on your own and figure it out?

Musician: Yes.

Director: And I take it you also learn as much as you can from your friends, and then you go off on your own and figure it out?

Musician: Naturally.

Director: And what about your professors?

Musician: Well, you do learn what you can.

Director: But?

Musician: But some of them try to tell you what your me should be.

Director: How do they do that?

Musician: They steer you.

Director: What do they use to steer?

Musician: The reward of their personal approval. And I have to admit. It can be seductive.

Director: Why?

Musician: Because you're dealing with masters of the universe of knowledge! Ha, ha!

Director: I see you're immune to this seduction. But what if someday you're not?

Musician: Not immune to the university?

Director: No, to a different universe.

Musician: What universe?

Director: The universe of music.

Musician: Well, I'll have an advantage.

Director: What advantage?

Musician: Right now I'm dealing with a universe I'm not much taken with.

Director: How is that an advantage?

Musician: You feel more free to make mistakes when you're not taken. And you can learn from those mistakes.

Director: Then you'd better make the most of it while you can.

Musician: Why do you say that so seriously?

Director: Because I'm afraid of what you'll be taken with.

Musician: Music?

Director: Yes, music. But something more.

Musician: What more?

Director: Your fans.

Musician: Why do you worry about that?

Director: Because of why you'll be taken with them.

Musician: And why will I be taken with them?

Director: Because they're taken with you.

Musician: So what do you think I should do?

Director: Make no mistakes that they can see.

Musician: Ha! Why? Because they'll no longer be taken with me if they see my mistakes?

Director: No, I was thinking something else.

Musician: What?

Director: You'll no longer be taken with them.

Musician: But why?

Director: Because the spell will break.

Musician: What spell?

Director: The one that keeps you enthralled.

Musician: How am I enthralled?

Director: You think you'll find in their eyes the me you're meant to be.

Musician: So what's wrong with making mistakes?

Director: When you do, your fans might not see your flaws for what they are.

Musician: And what's wrong with that?

Director: If they don't, you won't be able to help but wonder.

Musician: Wonder what?

Director: How well those eyes of theirs, that you depend so much upon — see.

7. HOME (PROFESSOR)

Professor: The university is a second home for many.

Director: What makes it this home?

Professor: The warm and nurturing environment we provide.

Director: What makes it warm?

Professor: Generous attention from the faculty.

Director: And I suppose that's what makes it nurturing, too?

Professor: Exactly.

Director: Who thrives best here? Students who come from a first home that resembles your environment? Or students who come from an opposite situation?

Professor: Well, those from an opposite situation will have much to learn.

Director: What will they have to learn most?

Professor: Trust.

Director: And when they do?

Professor: They'll be a part of our core.

Director: The university's elite?

Professor: Elite? No, they'll be humble workers for the cause.

Director: What cause?

Professor: The advancement of learning.

Director: Learning what?

Professor: Why, all the knowledge in the world.

Director: And that includes knowledge of self?

Professor: Of course it does.

Director: Of all the knowledge in the world, how much is knowledge of self?

Professor: It doesn't work like that.

Director: How does it work?

Professor: You can't have any real understanding of the world unless you understand yourself.

Director: And you mean the human world, not the physical world?

Professor: Yes, of course.

Director: Then it seems appropriate you made the switch.

Professor: What switch?

Director: We were speaking of knowledge but then you spoke of understanding.

Professor: Ah.

Director: Was that intentional? Is there a difference between knowledge and understanding?

Professor: Of course there's a difference. And I'll tell you how it's relevant here. Knowledge can be cold, but understanding is warm.

Director: Always?

Professor: Oh, nothing is always.

Director: What would cold understanding be like?

Professor: Like something we don't have at our school.

Director: Your university prefers warm understanding. And it prefers this understanding to knowledge. Yes?

Professor: Director, you know it's best to have both knowledge and understanding.

Director: Both, yes. But one is better?

Professor: How so?

Director: You can have an understanding with someone, but you can't have a knowing.

Professor: Ha, ha. Now you're playing word games.

Director: But doesn't this game take us to the core of your core? And isn't there understanding in there?

Professor: Well, I'm inclined to agree.

Director: And what's outside the core? Knowledge?

Professor: Yes, knowledge is outside.

Director: It surrounds and protects what's molten inside?

Professor: We're going from warm to molten? And what's this metaphor? Something geological? Knowledge is as a sort of mantle or crust?

Director: What would be better?

Professor: No metaphor.

Director: Then let's forget about cores. So tell me this. Do you communicate understanding with words?

Professor: How else?

Director: Well, there could be gestures, and certain looks, and your posture, and so on.

Professor: Of course. We communicate with our bodies all the time.

Director: Can some of this communication, this language, be violent?

Professor: All language can be violent.

Director: Even certain communications with words?

Professor: Yes, of course.

Director: How can we win the trust of those who've known violence, of whatever sort, at home?

Professor: We come to an understanding with them.

Director: What understanding?

Professor: One based on our showing just how gentle language can be.

Director: But is that enough?

Professor: What more do we need?

Director: To reassure them.

Professor: How?

Director: By showing our strength.

8. ROLE MODELS (PROFESSOR)

Director: Not only do you teach language, you're a role model to your students.

Professor: Thank you. But all of the faculty are role models to their students.

Director: So it's important who the university hires.

Professor: No doubt.

Director: Do you hire for both subject matter knowledge and understanding?

Professor: Yes, we do.

Director: Does that guarantee that students will be understood?

Professor: Well, that wasn't the understanding I had in mind.

Director: Shouldn't a role model understand their students?

Professor: Yes, of course.

Director: So you should hire for that kind of understanding, too.

Professor: True.

Director: And students, they'll go where they're understood?

Professor: Not necessarily.

Director: Why not?

Professor: Because we want them to go where their interests lie.

Director: Understanding isn't in their interest?

Professor: Oh, of course it is. What I'm saying is that a student might have an interest in chemistry but have a mentor in the classics department.

Director: So they'll get some outside perspective on their field.

Professor: Exactly.

Director: What's a good outside point of view from which to observe the teaching of language?

Professor: It could be any.

Director: So long as there's some understanding concerning the core?

Professor: The core of language? Yes.

Director: Well, this sounds good. But what if your students arrive with strong negative feelings toward role models from their past?

Professor: Why do they have these feelings?

Director: Because the role models never showed understanding.

Professor: But it's not a role model if they don't understand.

Director: So that rules out famous athletes and the like, people you only see at a distance?

Professor: Of course it does. You need to know each other well.

Director: So there's a risk.

Professor: What risk?

Director: The risk of coming close to others in hopes of finding understanding.

Professor: Well, yes, it's a risk to come close.

Director: What happens if we come close, realize there's not much understanding, and pull away?

Professor: Feelings might be hurt.

Director: Whose feelings?

Professor: Both parties might be wounded.

Director: So should we avoid pulling away if we can?

Professor: No, I wouldn't say that.

Director: Then your professors pull away?

Professor: I can assure you, our professors don't pull away.

Director: But shouldn't they, if the match is bad?

Professor: And wound the student?

Director: Is it better for students to pull away?

Professor: It is. It's a lesson they have to learn. But it might take some encouragement.

Director: Why?

Professor: Because they feel pressure to stay with the mentor they've got.

Director: But where does that pressure come from?

Professor: Only themselves.

9. Roles (Musician)

Musician: Do you know what I think is the best education in life?

Director: No, I don't.

Musician: It's playing many roles.

Director: High roles, low roles, and everything in between?

Musician: Yes! Exactly. That way you gain perspective.

Director: Is that the purpose of education? To gain perspective?

Musician: I think it is. Don't you?

Director: I don't know. What can you do when you have perspective?

Musician: Understand the relative importance of things. Keep a sense of proportion.

Director: And this will allow you to make good decisions?

Musician: Precisely.

Director: So the true aim of education is good decision making.

Musician: Yes.

Director: And a good teacher will place a student in many different roles.

Musician: Well, I wasn't looking at it quite that way.

Director: What do you mean?

Musician: The roles have to be real, not some sort of role playing in school, though I suppose that wouldn't hurt.

Director: Are you saying you're your own teacher when it comes to this?

Musician: I am.

Director: And you would learn from any role?

Musician: Maybe not just any. You need to avoid certain roles in life.

Director: How will you know which ones to avoid?

Musician: Sometimes you have to learn the hard way.

Director: What if a teacher could help you steer clear of the roles to avoid?

Musician: How would the teacher know which?

Director: Maybe a teacher taught the teacher?

Musician: And a teacher taught that teacher?

Director: Yes, and somewhere back there someone learned on their own.

Musician: Learning on your own is good. But I don't know about all the rest.

Director: Why not?

Musician: Because the message gets diluted each time it's passed along.

Director: So there's a difference between first-hand knowledge, and second-hand knowledge, and third-hand knowledge, and so on?

Musician: Of course there is.

Director: Would you go further and say that if you haven't played the role, actually lived the role yourself, you really can't know?

Musician: Truly know? No, you can't.

Director: So it's a question of what we want to know, what role we're willing to play?

Musician: Yes, but we don't always have a choice in what we play.

Director: Some roles are thrust on us in life?

Musician: Yes.

Director: Can we close our eyes and hope they go away?

Musician: Ha, ha. No, of course not.

Director: So we must embrace what we're given to know?

Musician: Yes, that puts it well. Embrace. But once you have, and you've learned what you can, you can't be afraid — to let go.

10. Critical Thinking (Professor)

Professor: I seek to instill certain habits of mind.

Director: What's the most important habit?

Professor: Critical thinking.

Director: What's the difference between critical thinking and mere thinking?

Professor: Critical thinking involves analyzing things more closely, carefully, thoroughly.

Director: In order to form a judgment?

Professor: Yes.

Director: And you can do this out of habit?

Professor: Yes, of course.

Director: But might that not be a bad habit at times?

Professor: What do you mean?

Director: Aren't there things not worth thinking critically about?

Professor: What's an example?

Director: Tonight's television schedule.

Professor: Oh, I don't know. That might bear some careful thought. You might learn some things about our society.

Director: Maybe that's a bad example. Here's another. The throw of the dice in a game. Should we be critical here?

Professor: Ha, ha. No, not about the actual throw. That's just chance. But you might think critically about the game itself.

Director: What the throw of the dice signifies? Who plays the game and why?

Professor: Yes, of course. Things like that.

Director: Is there anything we can't be critical about?

Professor: No. Critical thinking is a way of looking at the world.

Director: I see. But why does it have to be out of habit? Why can't we just decide to think critically when we want?

Professor: Because critical thinking is a way of life.

Director: And ways of life are habit driven?

Professor: They are. We do have to choose to be critical, at first. But, inevitably, the more we so choose the more the habit develops. It can't be helped.

Director: What makes critical thought a good habit?

Professor: It helps you get at the truth.

Director: How? By stripping away the false?

Professor: Exactly so.

Director: But is there any guarantee that when we strip away the false, the truth will remain?

Professor: What else would?

Director: Nothing.

Professor: That's an awfully bleak view.

Director: Do you want your students to be in the habit of seeing something when nothing is there?

Professor: I want my students to be in the habit of seeing exactly what's there.

Director: And do you only want them to see, or do you want them to say what they see?

Professor: I certainly want them to have the courage to say.

Director: Why?

Professor: Because then their thought can benefit all!

Director: We can think critically on behalf of others?

Professor: Well, I don't know if I'd put it quite like that.

Director: Because we all have to think for ourselves?

Professor: Yes.

Director: What's a good habit for a non-critical thinker to form toward that end?

Professor: The habit of listening to those who dedicate their lives to critical thought.

Director: Because if they listen enough they might be encouraged to think critically on their own?

Professor: Precisely.

Director: But before they reach that point, what would make them want to listen?

Professor: Their interest.

Director: How do they know what that is?

Professor: The critical thinker persuades them.

Director: And in allowing themselves to be persuaded, they take a chance?

Professor: Yes, they do.

Director: But the critical thinker, too, might have to take a chance.

Professor: What chance?

Director: Do you believe we all have blind spots?

Professor: Of course I do. None of us has perfect vision.

Director: What happens if a non-critical thinker sees a blind spot in the critical one?

Professor: The former must speak up.

Director: Why would the critical thinker listen to the less-than-critical?

Professor: You mean, why would they take that chance? Because the latter demonstrates to them exactly where they're blind. But then there's a greater chance the critical thinker has to take.

Director: Oh? What chance?

Professor: They have to take a chance on the fix.

Director: And what does that involve?

Professor: Breaking the habits that made them blind.

Director: But why is that taking a chance?

Professor: Because that might not be all that breaks.

11. Freedom (Musician)

Director: If you were a music professor, what would you teach?

Musician: Freedom.

Director: Why freedom?

Musician: Because freedom gives life to music.

Director: What does it mean to be free when performing?

Musician: You let yourself go.

Director: Can you let go in normal life?

Musician: You can, but it's not the same.

Director: So music is special?

Musician: Yes.

Director: Can you let go in composing, as well?

Musician: Of course. You have to be free to create.

Director: But free of what, exactly?

Musician: Conformity.

Director: So the free develop their own style.

Musician: Exactly.

Director: How easy is that?

Musician: Not very easy at all.

Director: Can someone teach you to have your own style?

Musician: I suppose someone can encourage you. But actually teach you? No. You have to come up with that on your own.

Director: So if you were the teacher, would you tell your students what things make for conformity?

Musician: Yes, I'd point those things out.

Director: With the hope the students would break with them, would become free.

Musician: Of course.

Director: And is it enough to point those things out, or would you have to show them how to break with them, too?

Musician: The breaking is the creativity. I could give them examples of those who broke. But they'd have to break on their own.

Director: Could you give them assignments calling for them to break?

Musician: I could.

Director: And could you grade them based on how well they broke?

Musician: Yes.

Director: But is music really all that simple? Just break a few rules and you're a success?

Musician: Of course not. You have to establish rules of your own.

Director: And if you're successful, others will follow your rules?

Musician: True.

Director: And then someone else will need to break them?

Musician: They will.

Director: So creativity is the constant play of construction and destruction? Or can it all be one or the other?

Musician: Well, if it's all destruction there's nothing left.

Director: And if it's all construction?

Musician: Everyone constructs new rules without breaking any of the others? I don't know.

Director: Why not?

Musician: To make a new rule is a creative act. But how much space is there for new rules?

Director: You're wondering what happens if we have thousands upon thousands of rules?

Musician: Yes. Won't it be stifling?

Director: So you're forced to destroy in order to create.

Musician: Right.

Director: Now tell me this. Do you have to know a rule in order to break it?

Musician: No, you can break it without knowing.

Director: Then why learn the rules?

Musician: What you should really learn is how the rules came to be.

Director: Oh? Why?

Musician: It's easier to break with certain things when you know their origin. And, besides, you'll learn certain creative techniques.

Director: But don't you want techniques of your own?

Musician: Of course. But some of us can't find what's uniquely our own until we've exhausted the past.

12. CULTURE (PROFESSOR)

Director: Do you teach culture, Professor?

Professor: Of course.

Director: In an entry level course or one that's more advanced?

Professor: Oh, I don't teach any one class on culture.

Director: Then how do you teach it?

Professor: The same way all the professors teach it.

Director: I don't understand.

Professor: The university as a whole teaches culture.

Director: The culture of the university?

Professor: Yes.

Director: What is the culture of the university?

Professor: One of critical inquiry.

Director: In other words, very important curiosity?

Professor: Ha, ha. I suppose you can say that.

Director: What's so important about curiosity?

Professor: If you have to ask....

Director: Oh, I don't have to ask. I'm just curious.

Professor: Then I'll tell you. Curiosity leads to discovery. Are you going to ask me what's so important about discovery?

Director: Yes.

Professor: Ha. Discovery is important because it leads to ways to better our lives.

Director: If we discover good things, you mean.

Professor: Even if we discover bad things, too.

Director: How does discovering bad things help?

Professor: We can learn how to protect ourselves from them.

Director: And all of this is what makes inquiry so critical?

Professor: Yes, that's true. Though 'critical' is usually meant in a different sense, the sense of the analysis of merits and faults.

Director: And analysis makes its own culture.

Professor: What do you mean?

Director: Merits and faults determine if something is good or bad. And the sum of many decisions concerning good or bad amounts to culture. No?

Professor: Well, I wouldn't put it quite like that.

Director: Why not?

Professor: Because you're forgetting the neutral.

Director: How could I forget? Things are either bad, neutral, or good — or some mixture of the three. Or is there more to it than that?

Professor: No, that's it, and it's enough.

Director: Enough for trouble at school, I'd imagine.

Professor: What trouble?

Director: For instance? The sociology department decides something is good. The economics department thinks it's bad. And you, you think it's neither bad nor good — and find yourself in the middle of a culture war.

Professor: No, no. That's just part of the process in our culture. People honestly voice their views, and listen to those of others.

Director: And when they simply disagree?

Professor: They agree to disagree.

Director: But then isn't there a sort of tendency?

Professor: What tendency?

Director: A tendency toward the neutral. If no one really takes a stand, isn't that what we've got? We all agree to disagree, so nothing moves forward or back.

Professor: Well, you might have a point. After all, inquiry in itself is neutral.

Director: Is it? If you inquire into something controversial, is the inquiry neutral?

Professor: If it's done the proper way? Yes.

Director: But if it isn't?

Professor: The inquiry might be prejudiced.

Director: Does this hold for mere curiosity?

Professor: I don't see how there's any prejudice in curiosity.

Director: Then where does the prejudice come in?

Professor: That's a good question.

Director: Still, you agree that curiosity should be the seed for inquiry?

Professor: Yes, I do.

Director: Can you teach curiosity?

Professor: You can awaken it.

Director: How?

Professor: By encouraging it.

Director: How do you do that?

Professor: You show how important it is to the school and its culture.

Director: This culture depends on students' curiosity?

Professor: Absolutely.

Director: So they become part of the culture that's founded, in a way, on them.

Professor: And that's the beauty.

Director: Would you say that as their curiosity grows, they become more themselves?

Professor: I would. Curiosity is a core part of self.

Director: But here's what I don't understand. Why can't they become more themselves on their own?

Professor: You can't drop a seed on rocky ground and expect it to grow. You need the right soil.

Director: And the university has that soil?

Professor: Yes.

Director: Are you sure?

Professor: Director, just look at our results.

13. MANNERS (PROFESSOR)

Director: In your university's culture, are manners important?

Professor: Oh, yes. Very much so. We all must respect others and be civil in our arguments.

Director: Why?

Professor: Because that's the kind of community we want.

Director: What are the advantages of a community like this?

Professor: People aren't afraid to present new findings or interpretations and draw tentative conclusions.

Director: So no one bullies anyone?

Professor: Not on my campus.

Director: That's good. But how do you prevent bullying?

Professor: We issue warnings when it occurs.

Director: To students only?

Professor: No, to faculty, as well.

Director: And if they don't heed the warnings?

Professor: They're expelled.

Director: Would you even expel someone on the faculty who towers in their field?

Professor: We've done it.

Director: I'm impressed. But, you know, it's one thing to discourage bad behavior. It's another thing to encourage the good.

Professor: That's absolutely true. That's why manners make up a portion of a student's grade, and of a faculty member's annual review.

Director: You take manners very seriously.

Professor: We do.

Director: But tell me something. Can manners ever be too good?

Professor: I don't see how they could.

Director: What if, for example, someone listens politely, but to a fault?

Professor: They listen when they shouldn't?

Director: Yes, they listen when they should object.

Professor: Well, yes. That's a problem. But when should they object?

Director: Don't most people object when they're shocked?

Professor: I suppose. But what's an example of something that shocks?

Director: Manners only go so far and then should be dropped.

Professor: That's not shocking. But how can we know when we should drop them?

Director: When they prevent us from getting our point across.

Professor: Ha, ha. I would have looked at it from the other perspective — when someone rude is trying to make a point. You drop your manners and tell them to stop being rude. But let's take it from your perspective. How can manners prevent making your point?

Director: They prevent you from reaching one who's asleep.

Professor: And rudeness wakes them up?

Director: Yes, like a splash of cold water.

Professor: And after the splash, you go back to being polite?

Director: Of course, once you have their attention.

Professor: But then anyone who feels he or she isn't getting proper attention will start splashing cold water around!

Director: There are worse things in life.

Professor: Such as?

Director: Drifting around in a fog of good manners, oblivious to the truth someone speaks.

Professor: And if this someone throws cold water but speaks no truth?

Director: Then we'll give them what they deserve.

14. INTERESTS (PROFESSOR)

Director: Do you educate students in their interests, or do they figure them out themselves?

Professor: We educate them in how to figure them out.

Director: And how do they figure them out?

Professor: By exploring various fields.

Director: What are they looking for as they explore?

Professor: Something that grabs them.

Director: Grabs them?

Professor: Captures their attention.

Director: So we're captured by our interests? History, for instance?

Professor: Yes. Why, you don't like that idea?

Director: I'm more inclined to say we should capture our interests.

Professor: The result is the same.

Director: Is it?

Professor: Why wouldn't it be?

Director: Your way suggests we're at the mercy of our interests.

Professor: And your way suggests our interests are at our mercy.

Director: Aren't they?

Professor: Director, it's not about mercy. It's about that spark.

Director: The spark that lights history aflame?

Professor: The spark that lights you aflame!

Director: So you teach your students to consume themselves in fire?

Professor: We teach them to have a flame they can tend.

Director: So when you encounter your interest, whatever it might be, sparks will fly and you should use them to light your fire.

Professor: Yes, that's a fine way of putting it.

Director: And to be clear, we're saying it's in your interest to have a fire?

Professor: Of course we are.

Director: What do we do with the fire?

Professor: What do you mean?

Director: Do we cook with it?

Professor: Ha. Sure, why not?

Director: Do we start other fires?

Professor: Yes, but carefully.

Director: Why carefully?

Professor: Fire is a dangerous thing.

Director: Even in our metaphor?

Professor: Even so.

Director: But how can that be?

Professor: If you light someone's fire, and the flames consume them, they'll lose perspective.

Director: If flames consume you, won't you lose more than that?

Professor: Yes, yes. But my point is they might think there's nothing more important than their interest, their fire.

Director: But what could be more important than that?

Professor: How they treat others!

Director: But they treat them well by lighting their fire. No?

Professor: Not all of them want our kind of fire.

Director: You mean they don't like history?

Professor: You know what I mean.

Director: I think if they knew fire like we know fire, they'd want it, too.

Professor: So we should all run around lighting each other's fire?

Director: Does that sound so bad? And maybe those students who light the most fires have what it takes to teach. But now I wonder.

Professor: What do you wonder?

Director: What happens if someone runs out of fuel? I mean, it can't be as simple as lighting the fire and then that's it.

Professor: No, I think you're right. People must find fuel.

Director: What's the fuel?

Professor: I don't know.

Director: What? You don't know? How can you teach?

Professor: Oh, stop teasing. Let's say curiosity is the fuel.

Director: But haven't you heard curiosity killed the cat?

Professor: Ha, ha. Yes, of course. But haven't you heard?

Director: Heard what?

Professor: Satisfaction brought it back.

15. Interests 2 (Musician)

Musician: I'm not sure I'd say you burn when you find something that interests you.

Director: What would you say?

Musician: You flow.

Director: And like all liquid things, you flow toward lower ground?

Musician: Ha, ha. The metaphor has its limits.

Director: Yes, and we'll say nothing of getting all dammed up.

Musician: There's no doubt you'll come across obstructions as you flow. But if the interest is true, you'll find a way around.

Director: Does this hold for obstructions in the mind?

Musician: Yes, especially so. Interest makes for fluidity of thought.

Director: Well, this all sounds very good. But what comes of flow?

Musician: For me? Music. For others? Whatever they're interested in.

Director: Can you separate what comes of the flow from the flow itself?

Musician: Are you asking if it's ever flow for its own sake? No, I don't think it is.

Director: Why? Isn't feeling good good for its own sake? Or doesn't flow feel good?

Musician: Flow is the most amazing feeling in the world! But it's not that we don't want flow on its own. It's that we can't have it.

Director: Flow exists toward an end?

Musician: Exactly.

Director: So, you'd advise your fellow students to find their end.

Musician: Without a doubt.

Director: And if they can't find it?

Musician: They're looking in the wrong places.

Director: How will they know where to look? Where did you look?

Musician: I heard a song on the radio one day as a boy and that was it.

Director: So you never really looked.

Musician: No, I just knew.

Director: And is that the best way to arrive at the end of our flow, just to somehow know?

Musician: The best way to arrive is whatever way you can.

Director: So if I look and look and finally find my interest, that's every bit as good?

Musician: Every single bit.

Director: What's not as good?

Musician: Being so bent on searching you miss out.

Director: We can look so hard we fail to see?

Musician: It happens all the time.

Director: Does this mean we have to be patient?

Musician: Very.

Director: Even though you weren't patient.

Musician: I was lucky. What can I say?

Director: Hmm. Is that what flow is really all about? Luck? Waiting for your luck?

Musician: There's some truth in that.

Director: So what should universities do?

Musician: Universities? Become places that concentrate luck.

Director: How can they do that?

Musician: By bringing together lots of people with flow.

Director: They can tell from all the applicants who has flow?

Musician: If the admissions team has flow, yes.

Director: Can a whole first year class have flow?

Musician: That seems pretty unlikely, Director.

Director: Then of those who don't have flow, who should admissions pick?

Musician: Those who have potential to flow.

Director: And who has the potential?

Musician: Those who honestly admire flow in others.

Director: But how can we tell they feel this earnest admiration?

Musician: We try to learn how they react to the products of flow.

Director: Your music, for instance.

Musician: Sure. We can give them a taste and see how they feel.

Director: But what if they just don't like your music?

Musician: Oh, that's fine. We can expose them to many things in order to get a sense.

Director: And if they like none of those things?

Musician: What do they like?

Director: What's the opposite of flow?

Musician: Freezing up. But who likes that?

Director: Those who have doubts about flow.

Musician: What doubts could they have?

Director: The doubts born of the fear there's nothing solid in this world.

Musician: And by freezing themselves solid inside they hope to change all that?

Director: Don't they effect a change?

Musician: Yes, but it's not a change for the better.

Director: You don't think we need something solid inside?

Musician: Of course I do. But it doesn't come from freezing our flow.

Director: What does it come from?

Musician: Our beliefs.

Director: But people change their minds about their beliefs all the time.

Musician: Do they? Maybe that's why they're tempted to freeze.

Director: Freeze their beliefs?

Musician: Yes, but that's a mistake. Beliefs should be warm, life giving things.

Director: And when there's warmth and life, there's flow?

Musician: Yes.

Director: What else gives warmth and life?

Musician: Love.

Director: What? Are beliefs and love cousins of a sort?

Musician: Yes, and love is the elder.

Director: You surprise me. I thought love is always youngest.

Musician: Yes, but if love doesn't come first, what good is belief?

16. Dreams (Musician)

Director: When you flow, do you dream?

Musician: Of course! You're living the dream.

Director: And so you can't tell day dreams from night?

Musician: Ha, ha. It all blends into one.

Director: What about those who don't flow? No blending for them?

Musician: Those without flow can have powerful dreams, the purpose of which is to move them toward flow.

Director: But isn't there one condition?

Musician: What condition?

Director: That the dream is interpreted well.

Musician: Well, of course. And I leave that to you!

Director: I was going to leave it to you. What makes me qualified?

Musician: You're a philosopher.

Director: Since when have philosophers interpreted others' dreams?

Musician: What do you think it takes to interpret a dream?

Director: Boldness.

Musician: And you think musicians have more boldness than philosophers?

Director: Of course they do. You people play your music far and wide, and any-one can hear and decide if it's to their liking.

Musician: And philosophers keep their philosophy to themselves?

Director: No, but philosophy generally isn't broadcast like music. Most of my philosophy happens one-on-one or with a small group of friends.

Musician: Would you say musicians are qualified to interpret philosophers' dreams?

Director: Yes, but the philosophers I know wouldn't believe the interpretation.

Musician: Ha! And why not?

Director: Because it's very hard to communicate a dream. So the musician would likely have bad information to interpret.

Musician: So why don't philosophers interpret their own dreams?

Director: But that's what they do.

Musician: Should everyone interpret their own dreams?

Director: I think that might be best.

Musician: And what about musicians?

Director: As interpreters? They're second best.

Musician: Second to individuals interpreting their own? And why is that?

Director: Because musicians are skilled in making pleasing sounds.

Musician: Ha, ha! Let me guess. The habit of making pleasing sounds will carry over into saying pleasing things to the dreamer.

Director: To please is to please. And sometimes we please when we don't even know it.

Musician: But is that the goal? To please?

Director: When it comes to dreams? Why not? Tell me. When do your dreams please you?

Musician: When they're filled with music. And I don't need an interpreter to know it. And what about you? Do your dreams please you when they're filled with talk?

Director: You've hit it right on the head.

Musician: I share the music of my dreams with others. Do you share the talk?

Director: Not verbatim, but in a more creative way.

Musician: Are you suggesting I'm not creative when I share?

Director: No. Why, do you think you're not?

Musician: Of course not!

Director: Would you say your dreams are creative?

Musician: Yes.

Director: And they inspire further creativity, beyond copying down what you heard in the dream, when you're awake?

Musician: They certainly do.

Director: Then I don't see anything wrong in submitting yourself to your dreams.

Musician: What do you mean by submit?

Director: Allowing yourself to be taken by them.

Musician: Do you submit?

Director: No, I question my dreams.

Musician: Maybe I should question my dreams, too.

Director: And make music better than what you heard?

Musician: Yes. What do you think?

Director: I think we can teach ourselves much when we improve on our dreams.

Musician: And if we can't improve on them?

Director: Because we lack the skill?

Musician: Or because they can't be improved.

Director: You mean, they're perfect? Ah, what would you give for a perfect dream?

Musician: But I've had them. Many times.

Director: Then be careful who you tell that to.

Musician: Why?

Director: You act as though you've never heard of the jealous.

Musician: Oh, they can't touch our dreams.

Director: How do you know?

Musician: Because I often dream right in their faces.

Director: And they can't tell you dream?

Musician: Oh, I'm sure they can. But they leave me alone.

Director: Why do they leave you alone?

Musician: Because they come to think I'm a fool.

17. DREAMS 2 (PROFESSOR)

Professor: We want to nurture our students' dreams.

Director: Why?

Professor: What do you mean, 'Why?'

Director: What's so good about dreams?

Professor: They inspire us!

Director: To do what?

Professor: Live them!

Director: And we're successful when we live our dreams?

Professor: Of course we are!

Director: And our success reflects well on the university?

Professor: It certainly does.

Director: Then the university has an interest in its students living their dreams.

Professor: Don't tell me you don't think that's good.

Director: I won't tell you that. But there are dreams, and then there are dreams.

Professor: Oh, I don't like where this is headed.

Director: Where is it headed?

Professor: You're suggesting we should encourage students to have practical dreams.

Director: In other words, we don't want them to be dreaming when they dream.

Professor: Ha, ha. And what's an example of such a dream?

Director: A student is fairly good at sports and dreams of being a pro. But there's no chance they'll go pro. Do we encourage them in their dream? Or do we gently let them down?

Professor: Okay, that's a good example. But things aren't always so cut and dry.

Director: What do we do when they're not?

Professor: Encourage them and see how far they can go.

Director: And they'll be happy however far they go?

Professor: Some will be disappointed.

Director: Some or most?

Professor: What's your point, Director? That we should encourage no one?

Director: What are dreams usually about?

Professor: They can be about anything.

Director: Yes, but aren't they often about achieving respect, renown, and so on?

Professor: True.

Director: Well, I would strip all that away and focus on the thing itself.

Professor: The thing for which they hope to achieve respect, and so on?

Director: Yes.

Professor: So the dream is simply to do what you dream of doing.

Director: Right, and I don't mean dreaming of being, for instance, first violin. I mean, dreaming of finding a way to play violin as much as you can. Then if first violin happens one day, that's great. But you won't be crushed if it doesn't.

Professor: But those who make it to first violin are often prodigies. Expectations form around them when they're young, expectations they'll one day take their chair.

Director: I don't like those expectations. Prodigies sometimes mistake them for their own dreams.

Professor: But don't you admit it's best when dream and expectations align?

Director: Why would I? What good do expectations do? Who needs that pressure?

Professor: A little pressure can be good.

Director: Good for living up to someone else's dream.

Professor: So how would you help motivate the dreamer?

Director: I'd check if what they say they want is really what they want.

Professor: And if so?

Director: I'd turn them loose.

18. Advantage (Musician)

Musician: Sure, education can give you an advantage in life.

Director: Over the uneducated?

Musician: Of course.

Director: But also over the less well educated?

Musician: Yes.

Director: So this becomes a sort of arms race?

Musician: Each side seeks greater and greater education? Ha, ha. I think it's true.

Director: What's the advantage? That you know more? Or is it that you have more confidence?

Musician: Knowledge gives you confidence.

Director: Yes, but haven't you heard the more you learn, the more you realize how little you know?

Musician: I have.

Director: Well, does that realization make for confidence? Does it make for an advantage?

Musician: It does if you're dealing with others who think they know a great deal.

Director: Why?

Musician: Because you know they can't know as much as they think they know. And that should give you some confidence, which is an advantage.

Director: But won't the others who think they know so much have a great deal of confidence?

Musician: I suppose.

Director: And you only have some confidence.

Musician: I think you should have as much confidence as them.

Director: Why? Don't you ever wonder?

Musician: Wonder what?

Director: Whether they really might know what they think they know.

Musician: Well....

Director: I think we have to engage with them to see what they know.

Musician: Most people don't like to be put to the test that way.

Director: Why, because they don't know what they think they know?

Musician: In many cases? Yes.

Director: But what's the alternative? To let them keep their belief that they know? To keep their advantage?

Musician: Maybe we were wrong about the saying. Maybe it should be, 'The more you learn, the more you realize you know.'

Director: And the more you know, the greater your confidence and therefore your advantage?

Musician: Yes. So it's an arms race in knowledge. And in this race everyone wins.

Director: Why is that?

Musician: Because a world with a great deal of knowledge is better than a world with little knowledge.

Director: Because the world will have so much more confidence and advantage?

Musician: Ha, ha. Because knowledge is good.

Director: Tell me. Do you need an education in order to gain your knowledge?

Musician: Yes, but you can be self-educated.

Director: Is it better to be other-educated?

Musician: I don't know. I think it depends.

Director: What's the advantage of self-education?

Musician: You can focus on what you really need to know.

Director: And other-education?

Musician: You can learn things you might not have thought of on your own.

Director: Do you need to attend the university to get other-education?

Musician: No, you can learn from everyone you meet.

Director: Then why do so many people go to universities?

Musician: Mostly? Because of the degree.

Director: The degree is an advantage?

Musician: Of course it is.

Director: It opens doors of employment?

Musician: No doubt.

Director: How does it do that?

Musician: Having a degree means you have certain skills and you look at the world in a certain way.

Director: And this affects how you interact with others?

Musician: Of course. And it's this certain sort of interaction employers want.

Director: And the better universities are better at teaching this sort of thing?

Musician: Yes, and they're better at giving you prestige.

Director: What's the advantage of having prestige?

Musician: People tend to give you the benefit of the doubt.

Director: You mean, they trust you know what you say you know?

Musician: Exactly. And what you're thought to know.

Director: And that allows you to keep playing along?

Musician: Playing along?

Director: When you know you don't know.

Musician: Ha! I think that's true.

Director: Is that an advantage?

Musician: Well, that depends. Would you say it's an advantage — to set yourself up for a fall?

19. Civility and Respect (Professor)

Professor: Some students come from a background that places little value on civility and respect.

Director: And the university values these things highly.

Professor: Absolutely. So when these students go home, they're torn.

Director: Torn? But the choice is clear, isn't it?

Professor: Of course it is! But that doesn't mean it's easy.

Director: Tell me. Do you admit to the university those who lack civility and respect?

Professor: Of course not.

Director: So these students from the backgrounds in question, they had respect and civility before they came to you.

Professor: True.

Director: How is that possible? Did they learn on their own?

Professor: That, or an exceptional person taught them.

Director: I see. Now, when a student like this arrives, they're warmly embraced and treated with the civility and respect they deserve?

Professor: They are.

Director: So why is the choice not easy?

Professor: Let's clarify what the choice is. It's your background against your new found home. You have to decide in your heart where your loyalty lies.

Director: And you can't be loyal to both?

Professor: To civility and incivility, respect and disrespect? Ha, ha. Of course not.

Director: But this new found home, it's only yours for four years.

Professor: Yes, but those years promise a lifetime of belonging.

Director: Not if you don't do well.

Professor: You mean bad grades? Well, you have to keep up with your studies.

Director: Yes, but tell me. What if your background gives you certain insights?

Professor: What do you mean?

Director: Insights your professors don't have.

Professor: Well, that's for the good.

Director: Is it good if these insights cause you to challenge your teachers?

Professor: There's nothing wrong with that.

Director: Not even if you point out things they think they know but don't?

Professor: That's to the professors' advantage.

Director: So long as you point these things out with civility and respect.

Professor: Yes, and so long as the professors are patient.

Director: Why patient?

Professor: I think you know why.

Director: By patient do you mean tolerant?

Professor: Yes. But only to a point.

Director: Because you can't tolerate the intolerable.

Professor: Ha, ha. Yes.

Director: So there's a sort of line that can't be crossed.

Professor: There is.

Director: And professors are authorities on exactly this line.

Professor: Director, that's true. But the line is important.

Director: Why?

Professor: Because it's in no one's interest for a class to collapse into chaos.

Director: Chaos? How did we arrive at that? Still, isn't chaos a good opportunity?

Professor: Opportunity for what?

Director: To bring civility and respect to the class once again. Shouldn't we let the students practice?

Professor: But if they develop a taste for such a thing, isn't there a risk they might long to bring chaos again?

Director: In order to bring order again, and again? Perhaps.

Professor: Are you willing to take that chance?

Director: The chance that there will be order, preceded by a brief period of chaos? I'm willing.

Professor: But what if the brief period isn't so brief?

Director: Are we still talking about a university class?

Professor: We are.

Director: Well, if brief becomes lengthy, I suppose the university will feel compelled to bring to bear the weight of its authority.

Professor: And will it impose civility and respect?

Director: I suppose it might create the semblance of these things.

Professor: But the semblance of civility is civility. Don't you agree?

Director: You may have a point. But what about the semblance of respect? Is it respect?

Professor: If it seems like respect, it's respect enough.

Director: You'd be satisfied with that?

Professor: Of course I wouldn't. But given the choices? Sometimes you take what you can get.

20. Pleasure (Professor)

Director: Do you know what I think makes education work?

Professor: I have no idea.

Director: Pleasure.

Professor: Ha!

Director: Why do you laugh? Don't you remember what we said about education and enjoyment?

Professor: Yes, yes. But education is hard work.

Director: Ah, afraid of seeming a hedonist. But isn't there pleasure in the work?

Professor: Of course there is. We work, but we have our fun.

Director: Are fun and pleasure the same?

Professor: Ha. That's an interesting question. I'm not sure.

Director: Well, let's forget about fun for now. And let me tell you this. I work, and I find pleasure in my work. Is the work of education somehow different?

Professor: No, the pleasure in education is just that way.

Director: Pleasure for the one doing the educating, or pleasure for the one being educated?

Professor: Both.

Director: What's the pleasure of educating?

Professor: Seeing someone learn.

Director: And what's the pleasure of being educated?

Professor: I don't like this 'being educated'.

Director: What do you like?

Professor: Educating yourself.

Director: But then what of the teacher?

Professor: The professor educates the students on educating themselves.

Director: And educating yourself is a pleasure.

Professor: Yes, of course.

Director: Why is it a pleasure?

Professor: It just... is!

Director: Because knowledge is a pleasure?

Professor: Yes, knowledge is a pleasure.

Director: What makes knowledge a pleasure?

Professor: It's satisfying.

Director: Because we hunger for knowledge?

Professor: Yes.

Director: Do we all hunger for knowledge?

Professor: No, not all of us do.

Director: Why not?

Professor: I honestly don't know.

Director: Without that hunger you don't belong at the university, do you?

Professor: No, you don't.

Director: What if you hunger, but not for the type of food being served?

Professor: Oh, if you hunger enough, you'll eat anything.

Director: But you don't want your students in such a state, do you?

Professor: Well, of course not. We feed them enough so they can afford to hold out for what they like best. But now the metaphor is strained.

Director: That's okay. Holding out is quite a luxury, no?

Professor: And it's a great pleasure, yes.

Director: Holding out is a pleasure?

Professor: I think it is.

Director: You surprise me. I thought you'd say breaking your fast is the pleasure.

Professor: That's no doubt a pleasure. But there's a pleasure in knowing you can hold out.

Director: A pleasure in knowing your strength?

Professor: Yes.

Director: Would you say knowledge of strength is always a pleasure?

Professor: I would.

Director: And is that what a university should do? Teach the students their strength?

Professor: I like that idea.

Director: But what if that strength is only valued within the university?

Professor: What do you mean?

Director: I mean, the strengths you teach, what if they don't transfer to the outside world?

Professor: Then I expect my students to change the world — to suit their strengths.

21. Pleasure 2 (Musician)

Musician: I enjoy nothing more than music. What do you enjoy most?

Director: Philosophy.

Musician: What is philosophy?

Director: Conversations tending toward truth.

Musician: Ha, ha! Tending toward truth? Why only tending?

Director: Because sometimes the truth resists.

Musician: Don't you mean people resist the truth?

Director: No, I mean the truth resists us.

Musician: Why would the truth do that?

Director: Because it gets a certain pleasure from so doing.

Musician: Ha! Truth has a pleasure of its own?

Director: Don't you know? Where have you been? Truth enjoys making it hard on us.

Musician: Why?

Director: Because it's selective in the company it keeps, and wants to weed out the weak.

Musician: And I take it there's pleasure in being with truth?

Director: A very great pleasure, for some.

Musician: And yet you don't say philosophy is being with truth.

Director: When you tend toward truth often enough, there's a chance you'll eventually succeed. But the success is fleeting. Truth will only stand us for so long. So tend toward truth we must.

Musician: Are you done teasing me now?

Director: I've only just begun.

Musician: Ha, ha! Well, let me tell you something. There's truth in my music.

Director: The truth of its pleasure?

Musician: Yes. And that truth never fights me.

Director: Oh, but it fights me.

Musician: You don't enjoy my music?

Director: I enjoy it only so much. But through no fault of my own.

Musician: Why through no fault of your own?

Director: Because the truth of your music pushes me away.

Musician: Ha! And what about the university?

Director: Will your music push it away, too?

Musician: No, that's not what I'm asking. I'm wondering what you make of this. Universities don't claim to push anyone away. They carry on as though truth is theirs to freely dispense with no resistance at all.

Director: Why do they think truth is theirs?

Musician: They're long in the habit of tending the sacred flame.

Director: But who discovers the truth that feeds the flame?

Musician: Anyone can. Like you philosophers. But I feel bad for you.

Director: You do? Why?

Musician: Because you discover but rarely keep.

Director: And so we rarely know?

Musician: Yes. And here's the proof. You always ask questions. If you knew, you wouldn't ask. Unless...

Director: Unless what?

Musician: ...you were being ironic.

Director: What's wrong with being ironic?

Musician: Nothing, so long as you're not disingenuous along the way.

Director: Disingenuous about what?

Musician: Asking when you really don't want to know.

Director: Well, then I'm immune to the charge. I only ask when I really want to know. And doesn't that make me a good discoverer?

Musician: What are you trying to discover with me?

Director: Oh, I've already discovered something good.

Musician: You have? What?

Director: That your mind is elsewhere, my friend.

Musician: Elsewhere? What are you talking about?

Director: You're not giving this talk of ours the attention it deserves.

Musician: Where is my attention?

Director: You've been wondering something.

Musician: What?

Director: If there's a way to make me like your music more.

Musician: Ha! I admit that was on my mind. Well? Is there?

Director: Let me tell you about my approach to music, any music.

Musician: Please do.

Director: I try to see its designs on emotion. And I take pleasure in this.

Musician: And that's all the pleasure you take?

Director: Well, sometimes the music makes me tap my foot.

Musician: Ha! Then I feel sorry for you.

Director: Why?

Musician: You never experience music in full!

Director: But what if I experience truth in full?

Musician: How?

Director: I look at the music with a critical eye and I appraise its worth.

Musician: And where do you see its worth?

Director: In its effect.

Musician: Yes, but what about its effect on you? Knowing that is the only way to understand its effect on others. You need to feel the music, Director.

Director: But why do I need more feel in my life? I have plenty of feel on my own.

Musician: Yes, but you want that good feeling music brings. Why resist?

Director: What if I tell you I don't want the music to cloud my judgment?

Musician: Ha! What's to cloud when you focus on feel?

Director: I suppose it depends on the feeling.

Musician: That's why you need a musical guide like me.

Director: Only good feelings come of your tunes?

Musician: No, I wouldn't say that.

Director: Then why would I listen?

Musician: Because only the best, the best of feelings come from my tunes! Ha, ha! And I know you philosophers. At heart, that's all you seek.

22. The Cause (Professor)

Director: What's something you value highly in a student?

Professor: Commitment.

Director: What does that mean?

Professor: Dedication to the cause.

Director: The cause? What cause? The cause of education?

Professor: Of course.

Director: So you must offer an extensive array of courses on education.

Professor: Well, we do have an education department.

Director: And everyone must take courses there?

Professor: Why would they do that?

Director: Because if you're going to serve a cause, don't you need to know what it is?

Professor: Yes, yes. But I want students who are dedicated to learning. And you don't need to take particular courses for that.

Director: But do you need to learn particular things?

Professor: Oh, why are you making this difficult? All learning is good.

Director: Even learning how to weaken the cause?

Professor: If we learn that, we might learn how to keep it strong.

Director: Then are we apologists for learning the bad?

Professor: Ha! Of course not. But everyone knows all knowledge can be used for evil or good.

Director: And truly committed students want to know the difference between the two?

Professor: All students want to know the difference between the two.

Director: Then you have courses on these things?

Professor: Every course teaches these things.

Director: To be sure, you're saying all students learn both the things themselves and their proper use?

Professor: Of course. Neither makes sense without the other.

Director: So your students are committed to learning both what and how.

Professor: Yes.

Director: Is it possible to learn the how before the what?

Professor: I suppose it's possible. But I don't know how effective it would be.

Director: Then your students always learn the what first?

Professor: Our students learn what and how in parallel. That way they're equipped for what they know, as they know it.

Director: I see. And what about who, when, where, and why?

Professor: Students need to learn those things, too.

Director: Which is the hardest to learn?

Professor: The why.

Director: Why?

Professor: Because why is complex.

Director: Are any of the others complex?

Professor: They can all be complex.

Director: But none more so than why?

Professor: None more so than why.

Director: Hmm. I sometimes think who is more complex than why.

Professor: There may well be occasions when that's true.

Director: Just as there may be occasions when who is why and why is who?

Professor: Ha, ha. Sure.

Director: Tell me. If someone is truly committed, can they learn these things on their own? Or do they need to come to the university?

Professor: People can learn on their own. But the university helps.

Director: How?

Professor: It provides support.

Director: And when the students graduate?

Professor: They're committed to learning the rest of their lives.

Director: But if they need a little encouragement, a little support?

Professor: They stay in touch with the school.

Director: Through donations?

Professor: Ha, ha. Yes, that's important. But they stay in touch with the heartbeat, the living pulse.

Director: What is this heartbeat, this living pulse?

Professor: Everything that's taught and learned.

Director: And your graduates have access to that?

Professor: Of course! All they have to do is ask. We're dedicated to finding them a way.

Director: Through lectures and other learning-themed social events?

Professor: Sure, for instance.

Director: And if it becomes more about the social than the learning?

Professor: Ah, Director. Healthy engagement in the social commits us to learn.

Director: Why?

Professor: Because no one wants to run out of things to say.

23. DRIVE (MUSICIAN)

Director: What drives an education?

Musician: For many? A belief.

Director: What belief?

Musician: That education improves you.

Director: Does it?

Musician: It varies from case to case.

Director: Why wouldn't it improve you?

Musician: Because you're driven by the wrong thing.

Director: What thing?

Musician: Ambition.

Director: What's wrong with ambition?

Musician: It takes the place of hunger for knowledge.

Director: Can't you have both?

Musician: I think that's rare.

Director: Why do you think it's rare?

Musician: Because many of the ambitious are driven by a desire for distinction, and knowledge is only a means toward that end.

Director: Knowledge should be your desire?

Musician: Of course!

Director: But what about you?

Musician: What about me?

Director: You have another desire — improving your lyrics.

Musician: Yes, but first I want to know.

Director: Don't all of the ambitious want to know for the sake of their ambitions?

Musician: They don't all want to know. Some want to seem to know. And knowing without seeming means nothing to them.

Director: And the same holds for improving?

Musician: Seeming is everything here, as well.

Director: But you'll seem better if you write better lyrics.

Musician: True. But I'll not only seem. I will be better.

Director: You'll have substance.

Musician: Yes, and substance is what counts.

Director: How do we gain substance?

Musician: By keeping the horse before the cart.

Director: What does that mean?

Musician: Knowledge has to come first. Becoming better, improving, is second — a possible after effect.

Director: So I could learn because I want to improve. Or, I could learn because I simply want to know.

Musician: Right. And if the latter is your reason, the odds are good you'll improve.

Director: But if you learn solely because you want to improve?

Musician: And you don't want to know? Then I'm afraid you've missed the point.

24. Extroverts and Introverts (Professor)

Professor: Extroverts tend to have more confidence than introverts.

Director: Really? I don't know about that.

Professor: Then why are they so outgoing?

Director: Maybe they just put on a bolder face. But you're the one who should know. You have lots of experience with all sorts of students.

Professor: True. So let me tell you about an interesting case. An extroverted student of mine told me what he believed.

Director: Believed? What did he believe?

Professor: That anything goes that isn't challenged. And that extroverts are more likely to push things as far as they can go.

Director: So did you resolve to challenge pushy extroverts?

Professor: I resolved to keep an eye on the introverts.

Director: I don't understand. Are you worried the extroverts will push the introverts around?

Professor: That happens. But, no. I'm concerned with something else. Do you agree that introverts hate inconsistencies, contradictions?

Director: More so than extroverts? I don't know. I think it depends. Maybe we should talk to some introverts and see.

Professor: Oh, just agree for the sake of argument.

Director: Alright. They hate them.

Professor: And do you agree that any time you really push, you inevitably run into contradictions?

Director: Inevitably?

Professor: Just agree again.

Director: I agree.

Professor: Good! Now, when an extrovert meets with a contradiction, what do you think they do?

Director: Mostly? They shrug it off.

Professor: Yes! And let's suppose an introvert starts to push and meets with the same. What do you think they do?

Director: More often than not? They brood. Is that what you want to hear?

Professor: It is! And does that mean they stop pushing?

Director: I suppose it does. But if they can snap out of it, they sometimes push, and push with very great strength. How's that?

Professor: Excellent. But their push, would you say it's strong enough to move the world?

Director: In order to right the contradiction? Yes. But it takes a great deal of courage, if not confidence, to take on the world. But why would they start to push in the first place?

Professor: Oh, who can say?

Director: You brought it up, so you should say.

Professor: Ha! I'll tell you what I think. They push because they're forced.

Director: Forced?

Professor: By loyalty to an extrovert friend.

Director: I don't understand.

Professor: It's simple. The extrovert gets caught in a contradiction. The introvert rushes to their defense.

Director: I still don't understand. Are you saying the extrovert starts to push, then gets stuck, so the introvert starts to push, as well?

Professor: Maybe it will make more sense if I tell you what kind of contradiction this is.

Director: Please.

Professor: It's a contradiction having to do with beauty.

Director: But beauty is in the eye of the beholder, no? What's to contradict there?

Professor: Yes, yes. But we all start out by trying to explain the beauty we behold.

Director: Why?

Professor: Because that's what humans do.

Director: I'm not so sure.

Professor: Just suppose that's what humans do.

Director: We're doing a lot of supposing.

Professor: Yes, but here's the point. As we explain we meet resistance. And so we try to prove our beauty is the true beauty, the beauty for all.

Director: And let me guess. Others find fault in our proof.

Professor: Yes, they find our contradictions.

Director: But these contradictions vanish from sight when others agree.

Professor: Correct. But introverts don't lose sight of them.

Director: And that's because they want complete perfection in beauty, contradiction free?

Professor: Exactly so.

Director: How do you help them with this?

Professor: In my class? I'm afraid I'm fairly hard on them.

Director: Why, what do you do?

Professor: I ask these idealists to lead the discussion.

Director: What good does that do?

Professor: It teaches them to handle attacks on their ideals.

Director: And if they come to handle them well?

Professor: They're inured.

Director: And they accept there's no perfect proof for beauty?

Professor: Yes.

Director: So these introverts learn to shrug like their extrovert friends.

Professor: No! They don't shrug. They strive.

Director: For what?

Professor: Not to prove in a formal sense, but to show. Show the beauty they see.

Director: And what does it take to do that?

Professor: A great deal of courage and strength.

25. Introverts and Extroverts (Musician)

Musician: Do you know one of the strangest things about music? Someone who's a complete introvert can step on stage and be the most outrageous extrovert.

Director: Why do you think that is?

Musician: It's the magic of the stage.

Director: Oh, I wouldn't say it's magic.

Musician: What would you say it is?

Director: Acting.

Musician: No, it's not acting. Haven't you heard people say they feel more natural on stage than anywhere else?

Director: The stage is their element?

Musician: Yes.

Director: Acting is their element.

Musician: Oh, why do you insist on this?

Director: Do you think they're acting in their normal life off stage?

Musician: No, they're not acting.

Director: And they're really not acting when they get on stage?

Musician: I'm certain they're not.

Director: Then this suggests something remarkable. Introversion and extroversion depend on context. Or shall we say performing on stage really isn't extroversion?

Musician: Of course it is! And yes, these things depend on context.

Director: Hmm. But what do you say about this?

Musician: About what?

Director: People who've never changed from one to the other simply haven't experienced a great enough contextual shift.

Musician: I think that's true.

Director: Yes, but now I wonder. We were talking about an introvert becoming an extrovert for a limited time.

Musician: We were.

Director: But what about extroverts becoming introverts for a limited time?

Musician: I think that happens less often.

Director: Why?

Musician: Because most extroverts don't see extroversion as something to overcome.

Director: So our musician friend sees life on stage as an overcoming?

Musician: Definitely.

Director: What do our extroverted friends see as an overcoming?

Musician: Surpassing their limits.

Director: Aren't limits a deeply personal thing?

Musician: No doubt.

Director: And to get at them we have to withdraw into ourselves?

Musician: Yes, but you don't have to be an introvert to look inside.

Director: Just as you don't have to be an extrovert to look outside?

Musician: Right. But looking and doing are two different things.

Director: Are extroverts more inclined to do outside than in?

Musician: They are. And introverts are more inclined to do inside than out.

Director: It seems obvious what we can do outside. But what can we do within?

Musician: Think.

Director: And compose?

Musician: Yes! We certainly can compose.

Director: Are composing and thinking related?

Musician: Of course they are!

Director: And when composition is complete, there's performance, an outside thing?

Musician: No doubt.

Director: And some in the audience will take this performance and internalize it?

Musician: That's exactly what I hope will happen.

Director: And if they take it in, will it prompt them to think?

Musician: A good performance encourages thought.

Director: But what if the music has no lyrics, no words?

Musician: What's your point?

Director: Don't we think in words?

Musician: Not necessarily. We can think in musical concepts.

Director: Don't you mean the musical concepts can stir emotions and memories and these are the objects of thought?

Musician: Well, yes.

Director: What good does it do to think about these things?

Musician: Thinking can put you in touch.

Director: In touch?

Musician: With yourself.

Director: Emotions and memories are ourselves?

Musician: A very great part of us, yes.

Director: How do we experience emotion and form memories?

Musician: Mostly? Through interaction with others.

Director: Who interacts more? Introverts or extroverts?

Musician: I suppose extroverts do.

Director: Do they have a greater amount of emotion and memories as a result?

Musician: Of course not.

Director: Why not?

Musician: Because introverts make more of the interactions they have.

Director: How do you know?

Musician: I just... know!

Director: That's not really fair to our extrovert friends, is it? Do they make light of their interactions?

Musician: They don't affect them as much.

Director: Again, how do you know?

Musician: If interactions affected them as deeply as they affect me, they wouldn't have the strength to carry on the way they do.

Director: So you identify as an introvert.

Musician: Does that come as a surprise?

Director: No, but I think you're one of those you talked about. You love the stage.

Musician: It's true. I do.

Director: And that's where you get much of the interaction you need. But there's something strange.

Musician: What?

Director: Interactions affect you deeply. So why aren't you overwhelmed when you perform? Is it because you're an extrovert when you do? Or is it because you're only interacting in a superficial way?

Musician: No! I interact with the audience in depth. More than any extrovert would.

Director: So why aren't you overwhelmed? Maybe you interact with them, but they don't interact that much with you? A clap, clap here. A whistle and a holler there. What sort of interaction is that?

Musician: Director, that interaction makes me strong.

Director: Is it the same strength an actor feels?

Musician: I suppose it is.

Director: How about a political leader, that same strength?

Musician: Sure. But my feeling of strength is much more pure.

Director: Because music is the one pure thing?

Musician: That's exactly so. That, and math.

Director: Yes, but math doesn't draw the crowds that music does. So what is it with music?

Musician: It's the connection that's made. The more pure the music, the greater it is.

Director: Can you say more about what you mean by pure?

Musician: You know. Emotionally honest.

Director: But aren't there plenty of emotionally honest but awful musicians?

Musician: Yes, but the music has to match the emotion.

Director: And when it does?

Musician: The crowd goes wild.

26. Perfection (Professor)

Professor: Perfection is the enemy of education.

Director: Why?

Professor: Because there's nothing to learn when you're perfect.

Director: Do you believe we all have something to learn?

Professor: Of course I do.

Director: But some believe they don't?

Professor: Yes. They rarely admit it, but they think they've figured everything out.

Director: So they see education as learning mere facts that support what they know?

Professor: Worse. They see education as getting in the way of what they know.

Director: How would it do that?

Professor: By obscuring the truth with myths, with fancy ideas.

Director: But isn't the goal of education to overturn myths and dispel fancy ideas?

Professor: It is. But it has a positive side, too.

Director: No doubt it does. But I wonder. Is it possible to overturn and dispel every bad idea? Or do we always have some bad ideas in us, no matter how good the education?

Professor: As I've said, we always have something to learn.

Director: I think that's true with positive things. But can you say more about the negative?

Professor: The mind is like a garden. We must constantly uproot the weeds.

Director: But if we've thoroughly weeded, won't the garden, if only for a short while, be perfectly free of weeds?

Professor: Yes, that's possible, I suppose.

Director: So perfection isn't the enemy of education.

Professor: Not on the negative side, no.

Director: And on the positive side are the plants we garden?

Professor: Yes.

Director: But now I'm wondering this. Isn't each garden unique?

Professor: Certainly.

Director: There are various climates, many sorts of soil, different sized plots, and so on, and so on.

Professor: What's your point?

Director: Certain plants are best for each, and only so many.

Professor: There's nothing profound in that.

Director: But then I wonder. Is it really only so many plants for the mind?

Professor: Well, that's an important question for educators, you know. At what point do we step back and let students take it all in?

Director: Yes. But I have a question about our metaphor. What's a plant? Is it an idea?

Professor: A plant is a cluster of concepts and facts.

Director: Can a cluster be perfect?

Professor: A cluster can be perfectly useful for a time. But no, clusters are less than perfect. New facts and concepts can render them obsolete.

Director: So education is imperfect because it teaches the imperfect?

Professor: We can say that, yes.

Director: And the point of learning the imperfect is that it's useful for a time?

Professor: Yes.

Director: So tell me this. The imperfect you teach, is it the truth?

Professor: Ha, ha. Are you asking if there's Truth with a capital T?

Director: Is there?

Professor: If a truth dominates a time, it assumes that capital T.

Director: But that truth is still imperfect?

Professor: Of course it is.

Director: But people believe it's perfect.

Professor: Yes.

Director: Hmm. If you're of the view that this truth is imperfect, and you're very strong, might you render it imperfect for all?

Professor: Yes, I suppose.

Director: Do we think that's good?

Professor: The truth about the Truth with a capital T is always good.

Director: Why?

Professor: Because it serves education.

Director: How?

Professor: It uproots a very big weed and makes room for better growths.

Director: The perfect Truth with a capital T is a weed? But don't you think it can be a beautiful flower?

Professor: It sometimes seems it is.

Director: But if a flower seems beautiful....

Professor: Well, yes, on some level it's beautiful.

Director: Isn't beauty the level on which you teach?

Professor: It is. But we need to learn to find beauty in the imperfect. Because the world is, and always will be — a garden of imperfections.

27. Good Enough (Musician)

Musician: If you add up enough 'good enough' what do you get?

Director: Something that's perfectly okay. And what's wrong with that?

Musician: Nothing, I suppose. But wouldn't you rather have something great?

Director: Great is clearly better than okay. But if greatness is what you want, why are you talking about good enough?

Musician: Because greatness comes with lots of good enough.

Director: Why do you say that?

Musician: Because I've seen the great. They focus on the important, on making that great. Everything that's less than important gets a quick treatment to make it good enough.

Director: Do you mean, for instance, a musician might focus intensely on making great music, but then give their wardrobe quick treatment so it's merely good enough?

Musician: Ha, ha! Often enough the opposite holds! But, yes, you know what I mean.

Director: Would you say it's impossible to be great if you try to make everything great?

Musician: I would. There's simply not enough time.

Director: So you need to know what's important. How?

Musician: I don't know. It's just one of those things you know.

Director: You really don't think you can learn?

Musician: Maybe if you spend time with a master. But even then, what's important for you will be unique.

Director: So the first step in education toward greatness is learning how you're unique?

Musician: I think the great already know that on their own.

Director: They know it from birth?

Musician: In a sense? Yes.

Director: So if you don't know you're unique, you should just give up? You'll never be great?

Musician: I know it sounds so cold. But I think it's true. Not everyone can be great.

Director: Then why do so many people write books, give lectures, offer courses on how to be great?

Musician: It's because our society is somewhat fluid.

Director: Can you say more?

Musician: People go from rags to riches, and so on. Others see this and think they can do it, too. And there are people who offer to sell them the dream.

Director: Hmm.

Musician: What is it?

Director: I'm trying to imagine what it would be like not to know you're unique.

Musician: Ha! Well, I agree — you're unique.

Director: No, that's not my point. Tell me. What's the psychology of sameness?

Musician: I don't know, either! Ha, ha! But how about this? You feel you belong with everyone else.

Director: If you're unique you only belong with certain others?

Musician: I think that's true.

Director: But what about your great musician friends? Don't they belong with their vast audiences?

Musician: Well....

Director: And if they could, wouldn't they have everyone as a fan?

Musician: That's not true of every musician, you know.

Director: Some play to a niche?

Musician: Yes.

Director: Who's greater? Someone with broad appeal or someone in a niche?

Musician: I don't think we can say.

Director: Really?

Musician: Alright. Here's what I think. Commanding a niche can lead to later, broader acclaim.

Director: So you think broader is better.

Musician: I do.

Director: What connection, what belonging, is there between a musician and a very broad audience?

Musician: The sharing of what's the same in us all.

Director: Oh, I thought it was the sharing of the uniqueness of the musician with all.

Musician: Are you suggesting the musician is great but the audience isn't?

Director: Shall we say that together they're great for a time?

Musician: That's the standard answer.

Director: Is it true?

Musician: Of course it is.

Director: So tell me. What makes an audience great?

Musician: Their enthusiasm, their appreciation.

Director: Are they enthusiastic and appreciative during a bad performance?

Musician: No, of course not.

Director: They're appreciative and enthusiastic during a great performance?

Musician: Yes. And a great performance is nothing without an audience.

Director: But I wonder if there's something you'd concede.

Musician: What?

Director: Which is the greater audience? One person who appreciates everything you do? Or many people who appreciate, between them, most everything you do?

Musician: Some appreciate this, and some appreciate that? But no one appreciates the whole except for the one?

Director: Yes. So which do you prefer?

Musician: Honestly? If I had to make a choice? I'd prefer the one. And that's more than good enough for me.

Director: Yes, but I know you. You fully expect you'll find an audience of more than ten thousand ones.

Musician: Ha, ha! It's true! I believe — no, I know — they're out there. And the most important thing, aside from making the music great, is bringing us all together.

28. MEANING (PROFESSOR)

Director: Professor, what is truth?

Professor: Ha, ha. That's not so easy to explain.

Director: How would you start to explain?

Professor: I'd say that it's something in accordance with reality or fact.

Director: How does meaning fit into this?

Professor: Meaning? Meaning should be closely fitted with truth.

Director: Why?

Professor: Because you want your meaning to be based on what's real!

Director: As opposed to imagination?

Professor: Yes. Or lies, or error, and so on.

Director: Can you give an example of a time when truth and meaning divide?

Professor: Sure. You might imagine you're a wonderful singer. This holds great meaning for you. But it's not true. You're no good at all. Truth and meaning differ.

Director: But your mother might find meaning in your voice.

Professor: Ha, ha. Yes, that's true. But who else would?

Director: So not everyone finds the same meaning in the same things.

Professor: Of course.

Director: Is it different when it comes to truths?

Professor: What do you mean?

Director: Can we all find the same meaning in truth?

Professor: We don't all agree on the truth.

Director: But if we did?

Professor: No, I imagine different people would still find different meanings.

Director: And for some truths maybe no one would find any meaning at all?

Professor: I'm inclined to think every truth has someone who finds meaning in it.

Director: No matter how strange or obscure the truth?

Professor: No matter how strange or obscure.

Director: So all truths mean something to someone somehow.

Professor: Yes.

Director: Then tell me. Is meaning something we should preserve?

Professor: Of course.

Director: Are all truths worth preserving for the sake of their meaning?

Professor: Well, that notion raises difficult questions.

Director: Why?

Professor: Because certain truths are ugly.

Director: And yet they're meaningful to some?

Professor: Yes.

Director: Now here's what I wonder. Are we drawn toward those who share our meaning?

Professor: We are, naturally, yes. And that's a problem.

Director: How so?

Professor: We don't always want various camps of meaning to form.

Director: Why not?

Professor: Because that's how we divide.

Director: What's the basis of the division?

Professor: Language.

Director: Because meaning occurs in words?

Professor: Of course.

Director: Not everyone agrees, you know.

Professor: What do they say? That meaning occurs in feeling? That's so primitive.

Director: What's wrong with feeling? I mean, if something makes me feel good, isn't it meaningful to me?

Professor: Yes, yes. But you have to ask this. Does feeling good give us meaning, or does meaning make us feel good?

Director: And you believe it's the latter.

Professor: Of course I do.

Director: Because meaning is the highest thing we can strive to obtain.

Professor: Yes. Nothing else makes sense in the end.

Director: But can we find meaning and not feel good?

Professor: No, meaning always makes us feel good.

Director: Are you sure?

Professor: Of course I'm sure. Why, can you think of an example when it doesn't?

Director: Let's consider what might happen in your class.

Professor: What might happen?

Director: Say you have a brilliant student who understands the meaning of your teaching exactly.

Professor: That would give me pleasure.

Director: Yes, but what if they argue against your meaning?

Professor: The student has their own meaning? That's perfectly fine.

Director: But what if their meaning is much more powerful, even to you, than yours?

Professor: I'd go over to their camp. And I'd feel good.

Director: You wouldn't let resentment get in the way of feeling good? Some would, you know.

Professor: I'm not them.

Director: You're not afraid to go where the meaning is most.

Professor: No, I'm not. But what about you? Do you ever resent?

Director: Me? No, I'm grateful when someone shows me greater meaning.

Professor: And when you show someone greater meaning, do you expect gratitude from them?

Director: I only expect they share this meaning, whenever they can.

29. Meaning 2 (Musician)

Director: Can there be meaning to a song that has no lyrics?

Musician: Of course there can! I write songs without lyrics all the time.

Director: What's the meaning of these wordless songs?

Musician: The meaning is up to the listener.

Director: You don't have some meaning you try to impart?

Musician: Well, there is a sweep of emotion I hope to convey.

Director: Emotion isn't meaningful?

Musician: Of course it is.

Director: So if you write a sad song, you want people to be sad? And this is meaningful?

Musician: It's meaningful to the listener because it calls up memories of the sadness in their life.

Director: And if you write a song of triumph, it calls up memories of triumph?

Musician: Well, yes.

Director: Why are you hesitating?

Musician: Because not everyone has memories of triumph.

Director: So they can't appreciate your music?

Musician: They can appreciate it vicariously.

Director: Through their imagination.

Musician: Yes.

Director: And even if they had experienced triumph, they might imagine even greater triumphs as they listen.

Musician: True.

Director: Then tell me. Can imagination give us meaning?

Musician: Yes, it can.

Director: But which is better? Real meaning or imaginary meaning?

Musician: I'm not so sure the two are always distinct.

Director: What's this? Are you suggesting that meaning might be founded on imagination?

Musician: I never thought of it that way before. But yes.

Director: So if a teacher wants to give meaning to students, he or she will stir their imagination?

Musician: It happens all the time. Imagination is a tool.

Director: So we have two tools here. The thing that stirs the imagination, and the imagination itself. Your music is a tool of the stirring variety.

Musician: Yes, I think it is.

Director: But who wields the tool of imagination?

Musician: In my case? The listener does.

Director: Are you sure?

Musician: Why wouldn't I be?

Director: Because sometimes the tool that stirs can stir too much.

Musician: And carry our imagination away?

Director: Yes.

Musician: But even if that happens, the music eventually stops. And then the imagination is firmly again in the grasp of the person in question.

Director: Why firmly?

Musician: Why not?

Director: Because the music might cause the habit of letting go.

Musician: Director, let's be serious. We can't really wield, or control, our imagination. It goes where it will.

Director: Then how can it be a tool? Does my circular saw go where it will?

Musician: How would you control your imagination?

Director: I'd reason with it.

Musician: Ha! Good luck with that!

Director: You don't think imagination listens to reason?

Musician: Not at all.

Director: Hmm. Would you say there's reason to your music, or is it simply irrational?

Musician: You know there's reason to my music.

Director: And you use imagination when you compose?

Musician: Of course.

Director: So how does that work? Does your reason say to your imagination, 'Imagination, let's conjure up a song'? And it helps imagination in this?

Musician: They work together, yes. But more often than not imagination tells reason when it's time to compose.

Director: So your imagination controls your reason?

Musician: Oh, you're making too much of this.

Director: But surely you'd say one gives shape to the other.

Musician: You want me to say reason gives shape to imagination?

Director: If it does, would you say imagination is the color and reason the lines?

Musician: I wouldn't say that.

Director: Why not?

Musician: Ha! Because my music isn't some coloring book!

Director: Is it better if reason is the color and imagination the lines?

Musician: We imagine the limits? But what if imagination knows no limits? What if it's color no end?

Director: Then reason has won.

30. Results (Professor)

Director: Professor, we should enjoy our education. Shouldn't we?

Professor: Of course! That's one of the goals, if not the goal.

Director: You really stand by that?

Professor: Well, we shouldn't make it sound too simple. There's much to say about the matter.

Director: What's there to say?

Professor: We need to spell out clearly what enjoyment means and involves.

Director: What does it mean and involve?

Professor: Ha! That's a huge topic.

Director: Bigger than the topic of education?

Professor: Much.

Director: Then let's limit ourselves to enjoyment in education. What can we say?

Professor: We can say that enjoyment gives you the strength to carry on your studies.

Director: Without enjoyment we go limp?

Professor: Precisely.

Director: So a professor must find ways for students to stay strong.

Professor: Yes, but there's a fine line here.

Director: Between what?

Professor: Finding things for them to enjoy, and pandering.

Director: What's the result of pandering?

Professor: No real education.

Director: And no real enjoyment?

Professor: Yes, it's true.

Director: But when there's real enjoyment, real education, what do we have?

Professor: Usefulness.

Director: The educated are useful?

Professor: Of course they are!

Director: To whom?

Professor: To both themselves and others.

Director: To educated others?

Professor: To any others.

Director: To the pandered?

Professor: Yes. They provide an example.

Director: An example the pandered will follow? I find it hard to believe many of them would.

Professor: Well, you may have a point. But the educated clearly serve as examples to each other.

Director: They're inspiration?

Professor: Yes, they urge each other on.

Director: Are they a source of pleasure to one another?

Professor: They are.

Director: That sounds like a good result.

Professor: It is. But we have to be careful.

Director: Why?

Professor: Education has its enemies.

Director: But we live in a land of education.

Professor: However that may be, there are enemies of the true education.

Director: So we shouldn't talk about pleasure as an end? Why?

Professor: Why? Ha! Who is willing to spend a great deal of money to educate someone toward pleasure?

Director: I would spend a great deal of my own money toward pleasure, the pleasure of educated company urging me on toward ever greater things.

Professor: Yes, but people hear 'pleasure' and they get suspicious.

Director: What would make them less suspicious?

Professor: A certain kind of result.

Director: What result?

Professor: A kind of potential.

Director: What potential?

Professor: Oh, you know what kind of potential.

Director: Then why not tell me?

Professor: Potential to amass significant wealth.

31. Pure Science (Professor)

Director: Does your university engage in pure science?

Professor: Do you mean science conducted without regard to practical applications? Yes, of course. We call that basic science.

Director: And what do you call science with a regard to the practical?

Professor: Applied science.

Director: Hmm. I'd make the distinction differently. I'd call basic science pure science, and the rest technology.

Professor: We can say that if you'd like. Though I think we'll ruffle the feathers of more than a few applied scientists.

Director: Because science is more prestigious than technology, and we're demoting them?

Professor: That's what certain people will think, yes.

Director: But it's funny. How much science would there be today if it weren't for technology?

Professor: Probably not much. Most people see technology as the end of science.

Director: And the rest?

Professor: They see knowledge as the end.

Director: The only end?

Professor: Well, there's also enjoyment, as with any learning.

Director: When scientists enjoy, are they having fun?

Professor: Some of them are, sure.

Director: Some?

Professor: Alright. Many.

Director: Do they need to justify their fun?

Professor: Fun doesn't need a justification.

Director: Not even when fun requires some very expensive toys? Powerful telescopes and microscopes, particle accelerators, reactors, satellites, incredible computers, and so on, and so on?

Professor: Well, all that is in the name of knowledge.

Director: And knowledge doesn't need a justification?

Professor: It depends who you ask.

Director: I ask you.

Professor: Here's how I see it. People value science for its use. But what's the ultimate end of use?

Director: I don't know. What is it?

Professor: The enjoyment of life.

Director: So when scientists enjoy themselves, they're only doing what everyone else does or wants to do?

Professor: Yes.

Director: And if they don't enjoy themselves in their work?

Professor: They're not doing what they should.

Director: So tell me. If you had a student who was brilliant in science, pure science, but enjoyed technology so much more — what would you do?

Professor: Are you asking if I'd encourage them to stay with science? I'd be a hypocrite to do so.

Director: Why?

Professor: Because my heart is in my work. And their heart is in technology, for whatever reason.

Director: Now what about the other way round? What if you had a student who was brilliant in technology, but enjoyed science so much more?

Professor: Is this student good at science?

Director: Pretty good.

Professor: I'd try to persuade them to stay with technology.

Director: And if in our first example the student were brilliant in science, but only pretty good at technology?

Professor: Well, that changes things. You should go where you belong.

Director: And if you're brilliant at something, that's where you belong?

Professor: Yes.

Director: Even if you enjoy something else more?

Professor: I think in some cases you have to learn what to enjoy.

Director: Is it your duty to teach your students to enjoy their brilliance when they don't?

Professor: It's the duty of the university as a whole. Don't you agree?

Director: I would if I could be sure of what brilliance is.

Professor: Oh, you know what brilliance is.

Director: Humor me and tell me what it is.

Professor: It's having an exceptional talent.

Director: And it's a shame to let our talents go to waste.

Professor: Of course it is.

Director: Because of their practical applications?

Professor: No, because we value the simple beauty of talent used well.

Director: Beauty for its own sake?

Professor: Pure beauty, yes. Haven't you ever been moved by that?

Director: I've been moved by beautiful things. But I think there's practical value here.

Professor: What practical value?

Director: Well, I'll tell you. I'm not always where I need to be.

Professor: Ha! Who is? But what's your point?

Director: Beauty leads me on.

Professor: To where?

Director: My place.

32. PATIENCE (PROFESSOR)

Director: Can you teach patience?

Professor: Yes, of course.

Director: Can you give me an example?

Professor: Certainly. Think of a poem. Most students try to rush their way through. And then they get nothing from it. But in class I walk them through slowly, lingering here and there to bring out the beauty and meaning in full.

Director: And if they're taken by the beauty and meaning they'll exercise patience when they read?

Professor: Yes.

Director: But not all poems are beautiful or meaningful.

Professor: True. And when we discover that, we have nothing more to do with them.

Director: Is it beauty and meaning that afford a student of mathematics, for instance, the patience needed to work through a proof?

Professor: Yes, and it's so in any field of endeavor.

Director: Would you go so far as to say anyone who finds beauty and meaning in a thing, anything, will have patience for that thing?

Professor: I would.

Director: And does it follow that those who find neither beauty nor meaning will be impatient here?

Professor: I think that's true. But let's consider an example.

Director: Alright. If I'm dying to read a beautiful poem I have at home, and some-one wants to talk to me, and won't let me get to it, would I be impatient?

Professor: Are you two talking about something less than beautiful and without much meaning?

Director: Yes.

Professor: Then you'd be impatient.

Director: But if I'm talking with someone about something of beauty and mean-ing, and this keeps me from my poem? Do I grow impatient?

Professor: No, you enjoy the conversation in full, knowing the poem will be there for you when you return.

Director: And if when I get back another such conversation awaits?

Professor: What a wonderful world you're describing! I think you'd put the poem off.

Director: But couldn't I do better?

Professor: How?

Director: By reading the poem together.

Professor: You're dazzling me! But what if the friend doesn't like the poem?

Director: I suppose that's the chance I take. Or should I just keep the poem in reserve?

Professor: Better to share and hope for the best.

Director: I like that attitude. But isn't there another side of patience we need to explore?

Professor: What side?

Director: The side that says patience is a virtue, even when dealing with the meaningless and ugly.

Professor: People don't say that.

Director: Oh, I think there are some who do. And if they don't, they think that way inside.

Professor: So what do they think? There's beauty and meaning in everything, if only we give it time?

Director: What do you think?

Professor: Ha! Certainly not that.

Director: Let's put it to the test. What's the worst sort of thing you can think of?

Professor: A vicious tyrant.

Director: Do you see anything beautiful in them?

Professor: No.

Director: Do you see meaning?

Professor: Well, that's a more complicated question.

Director: The question is simple. It must be the answer that's complex.

Professor: Ha, ha. It all depends on what we mean by 'meaning'.

Director: What if it means significance?

Professor: A tyrant is very significant in the lives of those they rule.

Director: And if meaning means purpose?

Professor: A tyrant can have a great deal of purpose.

Director: What if meaning means what's meant?

Professor: Ha, ha. But what can a tyrant mean?

Director: I don't know. I suppose it depends on the tyrant.

Professor: Yes, but should we have patience here?

Director: While waiting to know what the tyrant means? I say, no.

Professor: But what if we have no choice?

Director: I don't understand.

Professor: Of course you do.

Director: But I don't. When do we have no choice when it comes to tyranny?

Professor: When we're forced to bide our time.

33. Perspective (Musician)

Musician: I've been thinking about it. And I've decided. Universities can never teach perspective.

Director: Why not?

Musician: What is perspective?

Director: A true understanding of the relative importance of things.

Musician: Well, who's to say what's important to whom?

Director: So no one can teach perspective?

Musician: No one.

Director: Not even if the teacher and student are essentially the same?

Musician: What? No two people are essentially the same.

Director: That's an interesting perspective to take.

Musician: Why? Everyone takes it. We all believe no two people are alike.

Director: Then there's no such thing as an understanding, a perspective, that's true for all, or some of all? Each understanding is unique?

Musician: Yes, there are things that are true for all, or some of all. But, still, each understanding is unique, in its own way.

Director: So long as it's true to itself?

Musician: Yes.

Director: So we should fight for the truth of our point of view?

Musician: Absolutely.

Director: And then life is a war of perspectives?

Musician: It doesn't have to be.

Director: Why not?

Musician: Because perspectives can harmonize with one another.

Director: But perspectives — musical notes, so to speak — can clash.

Musician: True.

Director: So maybe we should organize the world into musical keys?

Musician: Ha! Yes, certain notes belong together.

Director: Agreed. But there's something I wonder.

Musician: Oh? What?

Director: I don't know much about music, but isn't there always one note in a key that all the other notes base themselves on?

Musician: Of course! C in C major, for instance.

Director: Doesn't that note, that C, give shape to the other perspectives in the key?

Musician: I suppose, in a way. But why are you asking?

Director: Because I want to know the effect of a key on individual notes.

Musician: Well, a note is a note. A key just limits its interactions with others.

Director: And how is it with people?

Musician: Do they only interact with those in their key? Not always. But for many, if they had their way? Sure, they'd stay in key.

Director: So let's be clear. What's a key? In what sense do we mean it?

Musician: When it comes to people? It's a certain group, a collection of certain perspectives.

Director: A certain group such as a nation?

Musician: Yes, or a certain group such as a social clique. There are many types of groups.

Director: Can one key get along with another?

Musician: Songs can have more than one key.

Director: But not two keys at the same time?

Musician: That happens, occasionally.

Director: Really? Then people from different keys can get along?

Musician: Yes.

Director: Even if there's a little dissonance?

Musician: Some dissonance can be good.

Director: What happens if there's lots of dissonance among two groups?

Musician: They'll either keep on clashing, or one group will go away to a place where it can harmonize nicely with others.

Director: What if the other group won't let go? What do we call people like that?

Musician: We call them bullies, tyrants, or worse.

Director: What can we do with people like this?

Musician: Employ some musical force of our own.

Director: Musical force? What do you mean?

Musician: We keep on playing louder and louder in our own key.

Director: Until we force them to let us go?

Musician: Yes.

Director: But what if they refuse, and respond by playing louder and louder in their own key?

Musician: Then we're at war.

Director: What happens in a war of keys?

Musician: Cacophony.

Director: And what results from that?

Musician: What do you mean?

Director: I mean, in war proper, people die. What happens in musical war?

Musician: People go deaf.

34. Philosophy (Musician)

Musician: What does an education in philosophy bring you?

Director: Usually? Trouble.

Musician: Ha, ha! Why do you say that?

Director: Because if the education is bad, as is often the case, you're left with a great deal of dissonance.

Musician: And if the education is good?

Director: Things are much more clear.

Musician: What things?

Director: Ideally? All things.

Musician: How do all things become clear?

Director: Through questions.

Musician: Questions you ask yourself?

Director: Yes, but also questions to others.

Musician: Is that a good bargain? Years of studying philosophy reduced to a bunch of questions?

Director: I suppose it depends on the questions.

Musician: Because certain questions are very powerful?

Director: Yes, they provoke a powerful response. And that can be useful.

Musician: How so?

Director: Take a very basic example. Let's say there's a great impasse at work. A powerful question can open things up.

Musician: Is that what philosophers do? Open things up?

Director: Yes, or at least they try.

Musician: Well, I think music is its own sort of philosophy.

Director: It opens up emotional blockage?

Musician: You put that well.

Director: Thank you. But is it true?

Musician: Why wouldn't it be?

Director: When does music appeal?

Musician: When it speaks to us.

Director: To our emotions?

Musician: Yes, of course.

Director: If we feel sad, does a happy song appeal?

Musician: For me? A sad song does.

Director: And does this sad song break up your sadness?

Musician: It can. Haven't you heard of catharsis?

Director: I have. But do we always experience catharsis?

Musician: No, gloomy songs for gloomy moods can reinforce our gloom.

Director: When does a song break up and when reinforce a mood?

Musician: I don't know.

Director: And you call yourself a musician.

Musician: Then you tell me, philosopher.

Director: To do that I'll have to talk to you in the language of philosophy about philosophy itself. Then you can consider to what extent music is the same.

Musician: Sounds fair to me. So tell me.

Director: First, we have to modify the question. When does a discourse break up and when reinforce a notion?

Musician: You should tell me.

Director: Alright. Critical discourse can help break up a notion. And supportive discourse can reinforce. But it's not always that simple.

Musician: How so?

Director: Those who argue can deceive. Can those who make music?

Musician: With the music itself? Of course not. Music is fundamentally honest, even if it doesn't reflect the emotional state of the composer or performer. But what do you mean about argument and deceit?

Director: Those who argue can pretend their critical discourse is meant to break up an idea.

Musician: Pretend? I don't understand. Are you saying their discourse actually lends support?

Director: I am.

Musician: Ha!

Director: Why do you laugh?

Musician: Because that's ridiculous! Next thing you know, you'll say those who make a supportive discourse can aim to break things up!

Director: What's so funny about that?

Musician: It's meaningless! It's like saying 'I love you' to someone you really hate. But who makes arguments like this?

Director: Underhanded sophists.

Musician: Can you say more about what they do?

Director: Well, to put it simply — they argue badly on purpose. A bad argument in favor of something is sometimes as good as, or better than, an argument against. And the opposite holds.

Musician: Well, that's only common sense.

Director: What does common sense say about someone who wants the opposite of what they say?

Musician: It says to give them what they say they want, and teach them a lesson! But this gets crazy very fast, once you start second guessing what people want and say.

Director: Does music ever get crazy like this?

Musician: Not in my experience, no. But now I'm feeling cheated.

Director: Cheated?

Musician: I thought we were going to talk more about philosophy itself!

Director: So did I. But we've seen a truth about philosophy, nonetheless.

Musician: What truth?

Director: Philosophy doesn't always lead to where you think it will lead.

Musician: Is that because philosophy is easily distracted?

Director: I don't know that I'd say that.

Musician: What would you say?

Director: That philosophy never lets an end divert it from its means.

35. SEEDS (PROFESSOR)

Director: When you teach something as general as language, what's the most important thing your students should take away?

Professor: A love for the subject.

Director: How do we fall in love with language?

Professor: How do we ever fall in love? It just happens.

Director: Yes, but don't we fall in love with the beautiful?

Professor: Of course.

Director: Then language must be beautiful in order for us to fall in love with it. Yes?

Professor: Yes.

Director: So how do you make language beautiful for your students?

Professor: Me? I'm no poet. I simply show them the beautiful language of others.

Director: What makes the language beautiful?

Professor: It depends on the language.

Director: What do you mean?

Professor: There are two basic ways with words. The political and the apolitical. And there are many subtypes for each.

Director: And beauty differs accordingly?

Professor: It does.

Director: So what's the beauty of the political?

Professor: Clarity when it's time to be clear, and obscurity when it's time to be obscure.

Director: What? When is it ever time to be obscure? Are you blushing?

Professor: There are times when it's best to be obscure, or at least oblique.

Director: Tell me why, and give me an example.

Professor: I'll give you the example and you can figure out the why. Suppose you're writing about political things in a land ridden with tyrants. Can you always be clear and direct in your attacks on them?

Director: Hmm. I don't know about these things. But what do your attacks accomplish if they're not direct and clear?

Professor: They plant seeds.

Director: Seeds?

Professor: Oh, don't pretend you don't know. Seeds of thought.

Director: Ideas?

Professor: Yes. Haven't you ever heard someone say, 'Don't give them any ideas'?

Director: Tyrants say that?

Professor: No doubt they do.

Director: But you would give them ideas.

Professor: I absolutely would.

Director: How does this relate to the love of language?

Professor: There are certain ideas we love, like freedom, and we communicate them through words.

Director: So we love language as a means, a means to communicate ideas?

Professor: Yes, the ideas are the ends.

Director: And the ends justify the means?

Professor: Ha, ha. It's true.

Director: So if we're planting the seed of freedom, we can say things in whatever way possible, no matter how crazy or strange, in order for that seed to take?

Professor: Yes.

Director: And does it work the other way round?

Professor: What do you mean?

Director: Do the means justify the end?

Professor: Ideas don't need justification.

Director: But language does?

Professor: Well, if we're talking about beautiful language — no, it needs no justification.

Director: So the saying 'the end justifies the means' means nothing here.

Professor: True. Beautiful language justifies itself.

Director: But what if the end of such language is bad? Is it still justified then?

Professor: Why would the end be bad?

Director: I don't know. But let's suppose it is.

Professor: The end of beautiful language is bad ideas? But that makes no sense.

Director: Because beauty leads to good?

Professor: Of course.

Director: Always?

Professor: Always.

Director: Because beautiful seeds sprout beautiful plants?

Professor: Yes.

Director: But I've heard of ugly seeds that produce beautiful growths.

Professor: Well, yes. There are such cases.

Director: And I've even heard of beautiful seeds that produce terribly ugly weeds. What? Nothing to say?

Professor: That happens from time to time.

Director: So we need to know which seed produces what. How can we tell?

Professor: By studying them closely before we cast them about.

Director: Yes, but how can we do that?

Professor: We can plant them in our own plot and see.

Director: You'd take that risk?

Professor: Oh, it's not so great a risk. If things start to look bad we just pull them up, roots and all.

Director: But how do we know when things start to look bad?

Professor: The same way we always know.

Director: Which is?

Professor: We keep an eye on the good.

36. Conditions (Musician)

Director: Can you make music anywhere?

Musician: Of course.

Director: Both in the sense of composing as well as performing?

Musician: I can both compose and perform even on the train, if I want.

Director: That's interesting. I would have thought you'd need quiet in order to compose.

Musician: Oh, sure. Quiet helps. But a true composer can compose anywhere.

Director: How is that possible?

Musician: You tune out everything but the music in your head.

Director: And I suppose it's the same with performing.

Musician: Yes, you just have to concentrate.

Director: And this allows you to perform despite adverse conditions?

Musician: You mean like hecklers? Ha, ha. Yes, I've had to deal with some. And my performance went on. Isn't that how it is with philosophers?

Director: I'm not sure I'd say philosophers perform.

Musician: Oh, I think they do.

Director: However that may be, tell me, Musician. How does all this apply to education?

Musician: Self-education or formal education?

Director: Either.

Musician: Well, let's talk about formal education. Can it happen anywhere, under any conditions? With a true teacher it can.

Director: What if one of the conditions is that the students are bad?

Musician: It's like when an audience is bad for a musician. You have to win them over.

Director: And what if the students are good but the teacher is bad?

Musician: There's nothing to be done. There is no formal education, then. The students have to learn on their own.

Director: And how do they do that?

Musician: They make use of the course materials.

Director: Books?

Musician: Yes. But it's very hard to have books make up for a bad teacher.

Director: Even when the students are off reading on their own?

Musician: Even then they'll have a bad time, unless they're strong.

Director: What do you mean?

Musician: You have to be strong to cut against the teacher's grain.

Director: You mean, the teacher can influence their view of the books?

Musician: Of course! And something like this happens with music.

Director: You like or dislike something based on what the teacher says?

Musician: It happens often enough.

Director: Why would a teacher assign a book he or she doesn't like?

Musician: They want to take it down.

Director: Take it down? How?

Musician: More often than not? Through critical theory. But the students need to take the theory for what it is, not what it's said to be — and to form their own opinion of books.

Director: What students do you think are equipped to do that?

Musician: The rare ones. Those who always read what's written — with their own eyes.

37. Hopes (Professor)

Professor: Working with students keeps me young.

Director: How so?

Professor: They're filled with hope.

Director: And that gives you hope?

Professor: A great deal of it.

Director: Hope for what?

Professor: The future!

Director: Your future?

Professor: Our future!

Director: Are you so sure you'll be a part of that future?

Professor: Director.

Director: I'm just trying to understand what you're hoping.

Professor: I'm hoping for a better world.

Director: One that professors shape through their teaching?

Professor: Do you doubt professors have an impact on the world?

Director: We all have an impact on the world. Why, are you suggesting professors have a greater impact than most?

Professor: I think professors can have some of the greatest impact.

Director: In what way?

Professor: They shape the way their students think!

Director: I thought they were supposed to teach students how to think.

Professor: That's a distinction without a difference.

Director: But what if it's the other way round?

Professor: Students shape how professors think? Ha, ha.

Director: No, but be serious. Can't you learn from your students?

Professor: Of course.

Director: And doesn't that change how you think?

Professor: Rarely.

Director: How can you learn and not change how you think?

Professor: Think about lawyers. They all know just two things — the facts and the law. Just because you learn new facts, nothing changes concerning the law.

Director: What you learn from students are facts?

Professor: Yes, and I am the law. Ha, ha.

Director: But can't the law change in light of the facts?

Professor: Yes, but that's up to the legislature.

Director: Who's your legislature?

Professor: The great thinkers, who else?

Director: You abide by their laws?

Professor: Yes. I have a lower opinion of myself than you might imagine.

Director: You really have no hope to be a great thinker one day?

Professor: Why would I hope that? I hope I get good students in my next class. I hope I'm of use to them. I hope they go off and do great things.

Director: And make the world a better place?

Professor: Yes! Do you think I'm unrealistic?

Director: I don't know. But I want to know one thing.

Professor: What?

Director: What do you think great thinkers hope?

Professor: To be understood.

Director: Why, do they have trouble being clear?

Professor: Ha, ha! Of course they do!

Director: Is it the struggle to be clear that makes them great?

Professor: Many people struggle to be clear, and they're not great.

Director: Then what makes the great great?

Professor: Success.

38. Common Ground (Musician)

Musician: It's not always easy to communicate musical ideas.

Director: There are musical ideas?

Musician: Oh, don't pretend you don't know.

Director: But what's an idea?

Musician: You tell me.

Director: I'll tell you what I once heard. Ideas are beliefs that cause a way of thinking. But what does that mean here? Do we have to believe in music? Does it make us think a certain way when we do?

Musician: You always have to be exact, don't you? Well, musical ideas and.... What shall we call the other types of ideas?

Director: Intellectual ideas?

Musician: No, music exercises the intellect.

Director: I thought music exercised the emotions.

Musician: Where do you think the emotions live?

Director: Let's just say an idea is an idea.

Musician: Fine.

Director: So do we have to believe in music?

Musician: I don't know. What do you think?

Director: I'm not sure there's much to believe. We hear and we feel.

Musician: But not everyone feels.

Director: True. Is that because they don't believe?

Musician: Maybe it is.

Director: But what do they need to believe?

Musician: In the power of music.

Director: But if they don't feel that power?

Musician: Maybe they don't feel it because they lack common ground.

Director: Common ground with the musician?

Musician: Yes.

Director: And common ground can make us feel and therefore believe?

Musician: Oh, Director, what does it matter? As a musician, I just want the audience to appreciate the beauty.

Director: But suppose you wanted to win a convert. What would you do?

Musician: Well, since music doesn't exist in a vacuum, I'd socialize the music with them.

Director: That's funny. Professor says language is a social phenomenon. He also says it's associative.

Musician: And it's true.

Director: So how do you socialize music?

Musician: First, you teach the would-be convert about the musician.

Director: You teach biography?

Musician: Yes.

Director: And this includes learning about the musician's society?

Musician: Of course.

Director: And what about the musician's contemporaries, their fellow artists?

Musician: It certainly doesn't hurt to learn about them.

Director: So, now that we've got some context, and possibly some common ground — we turn to the musician's body of work?

Musician: We do.

Director: And this is our best chance for someone to appreciate the beauty.

Musician: It's the best chance I know.

Director: Is this so with literature or any other form of art?

Musician: I don't see why not.

Director: And the artist, what do they need to learn?

Musician: What do you mean?

Director: Don't they need to learn these same things?

Musician: About the convert?

Director: Or the people in the audience at large.

Musician: There are a lot of people in the audience, Director.

Director: But the artist can learn about the ones he or she meets. Yes?

Musician: True. But there's one important difference. For the most part, these people won't have a body of work.

Director: No? Don't we all have deeds we perform?

Musician: Non-artistic deeds?

Director: Yes. And aren't deeds our works?

Musician: I suppose you have a point.

Director: Yes. So what happens when each has context for the other?

Musician: Are you asking if they'll have common ground? Not always, I'm afraid.

Director: And when that's the case, what's the most we can hope?

Musician: That we achieve a mutual formal understanding.

Director: What's wrong with that?

Musician: Neither feels the other.

Director: And musical ideas are all about feel. But what about other sorts of ideas?

Musician: They're about understanding.

Director: I'm inclined to agree. But listen to us! Didn't we say an idea's an idea?

Musician: So you think we feel these other ideas?

Director: Or we understand the musical ones. Or ideas aren't ideas. So tell me. Do you agree that both feeling and understanding can give us pleasure?

Musician: Of course.

Director: Which gives the greater pleasure, the feeling or understanding of musical ideas, or the understanding or feeling of other ideas?

Musician: Ha! There's no question here. Music gives the greater pleasure.

Director: Why?

Musician: It just... does!

Director: And if you met someone who took exception to your eloquent argument in defense of your work?

Musician: The first thing I'd do is search for a heartbeat — because they might be dead! Ha, ha!

Director: Well, here, while you're laughing — take my wrist and feel for a pulse.

Musician: Why? Are you one of the might-be-dead?

Director: I am. And yet I'm alive.

39. HIERARCHY (PROFESSOR)

Professor: Are the arts equal? We certainly teach them as if they were.

Director: Do you believe there's a hierarchy?

Professor: Of course. And guess what's at top.

Director: Language.

Professor: Yes.

Director: But language can be many things. It can be poetry, philosophy, technical writing, and so on. Are they all at the top?

Professor: Poetry is the top of the top.

Director: Why?

Professor: Because of its beauty.

Director: You don't think philosophy is beautiful?

Professor: Philosophy is useful. But as for beauty? It can't compare. It lacks the music of words.

Director: But isn't music problematic?

Professor: Why would you say that?

Director: Because poets have to be careful not to let the music get in the way.

Professor: In the way of what?

Director: The clear presentation of ideas.

Professor: What poet would obscure their meaning in favor of a musical way with words?

Director: A bad poet.

Professor: Why would they do it?

Director: I don't know. Maybe the music is stuck in their head? Or maybe they're playing to the crowd.

Professor: The crowd prefers the music of the poem to clear ideas?

Director: Do you think it's the other way round?

Professor: But the music itself needs clear ideas.

Director: Why?

Professor: Because if the ideas aren't clear, that's a distraction.

Director: Or an invitation to let music rule.

Professor: Ha, ha. Yes. But at best, music should play a supporting role, as in a film.

Director: And what of those who prefer the support?

Professor: They might miss out on the plot, with their focus on the tune.

Director: Have you seen that happen?

Professor: I have. And not just with poems or films.

Director: Where else have you seen it?

Professor: In life.

40. PROGRESS (PROFESSOR)

Professor: This stupid computer!

Director: What's wrong?

Professor: The progress bar is driving me crazy again. One minute it says there are thirty seconds left to complete the task, and then the next minute it says it will take an hour!

Director: Why not just let it do its thing and come back later?

Professor: Because I have things I need to do now!

Director: You know, this gives me an idea for your next assignment.

Professor: An assignment for my class? What's the idea?

Director: Use the progress bar as a metaphor to describe real world progress.

Professor: Ha, ha. You never know when your work will be finished?

Director: Right. Sometimes it seems like you're almost there, and then suddenly it seems like you're very far away.

Professor: That's how it is.

Director: Tell me. What progress do you strive to achieve?

Professor: I try to awaken my students to beauty.

Director: And once awake they stay awake? The progress is complete?

Professor: It's not that simple. The progress is never complete.

Director: But you see more beauty when you're five seconds away than you do when you're five hours?

Professor: Yes.

Director: How far away are you?

Professor: Me? I'd say for some things I'm a minute away but for others several days.

Director: And if you go from days to minutes you've made great progress.

Professor: Of course. But if we drop the metaphor, we'll see some awakening takes years, decades.

Director: Is awakening the only sort of progress?

Professor: It's the only progress worth taking seriously.

Director: Can we awaken on our own? Or does someone have to rouse us?

Professor: Someone has to rouse us. Because when we're asleep, we just slumber on.

Director: But what if an accident occurs that awakens us with no help from others?

Professor: What, you mean like you fall out of bed?

Director: Sure, something like that. Couldn't that happen?

Professor: I suppose it could. But the point is the same. And our sleeping metaphor is wearing thin.

Director: Oh, but let's have some fun with it. And let's say we sleep and awaken every day.

Professor: Each morning we crawl out of bed, barely awake?

Director: Yes, and then we have some coffee and feel a little better.

Professor: And then we go to class where we're still a little groggy.

Director: Right. And then the professor says something interesting, and we perk right up.

Professor: That's fine with me. But to get a broader picture, we should talk about things like narcolepsy.

Director: Narcolepsy?

Professor: You know, the tendency to fall asleep wherever you are when you're relaxed. It's more common than you think.

Director: I'll take your word for it. But tell me. What do we want to be wakeful toward? Is it just beauty, or is it all things?

Professor: It's good to be wakeful toward all.

Director: So while a progress bar simply runs from asleep to awake, maybe there's more than one bar?

Professor: Yes, that's a good point. You can be awake in one thing and asleep in another.

Director: But never fully awake?

Professor: Never.

Director: Hmm. When we're more or less awake to something, what do we often feel the need to do?

Professor: I don't know. What?

Director: Judge.

Professor: Judge the thing in question?

Director: Yes. Isn't there an urge to decide if something is good or bad?

Professor: I suppose. But I don't like the idea of being half awake when we do.

Director: So what are the alternatives? Find a way to be fully awake, or never judge?

Professor: We can pass a qualified judgment.

Director: Qualified as in not absolute?

Professor: A provisional judgment, yes — to be revisited when we progress.

Director: And when we've progressed as far as we can?

Professor: But how do we know how far we can go?

Director: So our judgments should always be provisional?

Professor: Yes.

Director: And when we need to act on them? Can actions be provisional, too?

Professor: Of course not. But if we act knowing we might be wrong, we're likely to work less harm.

Director: What do we tell those who say, 'If you think you might be wrong, you undermine the act'?

Professor: We tell them you can have your doubts and act to good effect. It only takes some pluck.

41. LITERACY (MUSICIAN)

Director: Tell me, Musician. What is literacy?

Musician: The ability to read and write.

Director: Are some more literate than others?

Musician: Can some read better or write better than others? Yes, of course.

Director: What does it take to write better?

Musician: To be more clear.

Director: More clear about what?

Musician: Whatever you're writing about.

Director: Are you a better writer if you're clear about easy things or difficult things?

Musician: I don't know.

Director: Why not?

Musician: Because sometimes the things that seem easy are the hardest of all.

Director: Are you a better writer if you're clear about easy seeming things that are easy, or easy seeming things that are hard?

Musician: Ha, ha. Easy seeming things that are hard.

Director: And what about reading? What does it take to be better at that?

Musician: To grasp the things that are hard.

Director: What if the author of hard things isn't a very good writer?

Musician: Then you can't expect to grasp the meaning.

Director: Can you always expect to grasp the meaning if the author writes well?

Musician: Of course not.

Director: Why not?

Musician: Suppose an author writes well about something that requires detailed technical knowledge to understand. And you don't have that knowledge. You can't expect to grasp the meaning.

Director: Does that make you a bad reader?

Musician: No! You might be a very good reader. But not on this subject.

Director: What happens if we drop the technical from knowledge?

Musician: What do you mean?

Director: Suppose an author writes well about something that requires knowledge, non-technical knowledge, to understand. Are you a bad reader if you don't grasp the meaning?

Musician: It's the same as with technical knowledge. You might be a good reader but lack the particular knowledge required.

Director: Do you think it's the author's duty to give the reader the knowledge it takes to understand?

Musician: Yes, and I think that's an excellent point.

Director: Yes, but now I wonder.

Musician: What do you wonder?

Director: Are knowledge and experience different things?

Musician: They are. But what's to wonder in that?

Director: This. Which do you need in order to understand?

Musician: To truly understand? I think you need both.

Director: So I can know, for instance, what it means to stand out in the cold. And the author can give an excellent description of that. But if I've never been out in the cold myself, if I lack the experience, can I truly understand the author?

Musician: Before we answer we have to acknowledge a problem.

Director: What problem?

Musician: The author might lack the experience, too. The writing might be based on imagination.

Director: So neither author nor reader truly understands?

Musician: Maybe so. But I think that's as much as we can say about this.

Director: Okay. So what about music? Is there a literacy there?

Musician: Of course there is.

Director: Music can be written and read.

Musician: That's the way of it.

Director: But reading can mean two things, can't it?

Musician: Sure. There's reading music from a score, the literal reading of music. And then there's listening.

Director: Let's focus on listening. What does it take to listen well?

Musician: To see how the parts relate to the whole.

Director: What's the whole?

Musician: Your overall impression of the piece.

Director: Your emotional reaction?

Musician: Yes.

Director: So you have to see how each part affects you.

Musician: Of course.

Director: But really, Musician, how could you not?

Musician: Some people don't analyze what they hear.

Director: And they don't analyze how they feel?

Musician: True.

Director: We're making it sound as if music allows you to explore yourself.

Musician: And it does.

Director: Can't books do the same?

Musician: You know they can.

Director: Then tell me. When you write music, do you want it to affect people in a certain way?

Musician: I do.

Director: And those who feel what you want them to feel, they're the good listeners?

Musician: I suppose.

Director: Does an author want their readers to feel a certain way?

Musician: Probably so.

Director: So the reader not only has to grasp the meaning of the work, which is no small thing, but, as with music, has to analyze how they feel?

Musician: I agree.

Director: So is reading more work than listening?

Musician: I won't go along with that.

Director: Why not?

Musician: Because listening can be something more. If you have experience listening, you'll see how a piece relates to previous pieces, how it comments on them, how it goes beyond them — and you'll see what it says about how you should feel about it all.

Director: Is it the same if you have much experience reading?

Musician: Well... yes.

Director: Can we call this having a sense of history?

Musician: Why not?

Director: Do we need this sense in order to read or listen well?

Musician: No, we don't. It's an advanced sense.

Director: Who needs this sense?

Musician: I don't know if they need it, but it tends to develop in those who've always loved to listen or read.

Director: Do you think this sense can interfere with grasping something for what it is?

Musician: How would it do that?

Director: Instead of focusing on what it is, you try to put it in its place.

Musician: Its historical place? The tradition to which it belongs? But how can you know that if you don't know what it is?

Director: That's the question.

Musician: Well, people do get ahead of themselves.

Director: And when they do?

Musician: They misunderstand the work.

42. LANGUAGES (PROFESSOR)

Director: How does learning a language open your mind?

Professor: It teaches you there are other ways of thinking about things.

Director: Other ways of, or different words for?

Professor: Different words are other ways.

Director: Words are ways?

Professor: Of course.

Director: And when you have different words and other ways, what have you got?

Professor: Flexibility.

Director: And that's what you train your students to be? Flexible?

Professor: No doubt.

Director: But flexible in what?

Professor: Why, everything.

Director: What good is flexibility in everything?

Professor: You can bend but never break.

Director: There's nothing worth breaking for in life?

Professor: Why would you want to break? You can resist, and bend, and strain — but you don't have to break.

Director: But, still, we think of breaking as good.

Professor: What are you talking about?

Director: Think of breaking a horse. That's a good thing, no?

Professor: I prefer to think of it as training a horse — and yes, training is good.

Director: But we're talking about the same thing, aren't we?

Professor: Not really. Breaking is a violent act. Training is gentle.

Director: I'm not sure all training is gentle. But one word emphasizes one thing, the other another?

Professor: Correct.

Director: And these words differ in the level of cooperation they imply.

Professor: Yes.

Director: Do the flexible always cooperate?

Professor: No, they don't.

Director: They resist and bend, and resist and bend?

Professor: Right.

Director: Do they ever have to draw a clear line?

Professor: Yes, they have to draw a clear line at times.

Director: Why not draw clear lines all of the time?

Professor: Because then they wouldn't be flexible!

Director: Hmm. I wonder about the languages we choose to learn.

Professor: What are you wondering?

Director: If some of them are inherently more flexible than others.

Professor: Yes, some of them are.

Director: How do we know which ones are?

Professor: Look to the character of the people who speak them. That's a sure guide.

Director: The character of the people as a whole?

Professor: Yes.

Director: So if a people seems inflexible, chances are their language will be, too?

Professor: That's right.

Director: And if they seem very flexible?

Professor: Then their language will be much more difficult, but that much more of a pleasure to learn.

43. Mother Tongue (Professor)

Professor: A common language helps globalization.

Director: I can think of another way to help.

Professor: How?

Director: Through a translator class.

Professor: A translator class? So there'd be no need to learn a common tongue?

Director: Right.

Professor: But surely it's better for people to learn.

Director: Maybe if everyone were learning.

Professor: What do you mean?

Director: Is a common language the first language for some but not others?

Professor: Yes.

Director: So some have to learn it while others just know it.

Professor: Well, we all have to learn it at some point. But I know what you mean.

Director: Would it be better if everyone just knew it as their mother tongue?

Professor: And that's the only tongue they know? Of course not.

Director: Why not?

Professor: We lose diversity that way.

Director: What's good about diversity?

Professor: It opens up possibilities.

Director: Then native speakers of the common would do well to learn another tongue.

Professor: Ha, ha. I love how you act as though you've discovered something profound. But tell me more about this translator class you mentioned. Is it something like a medieval guild?

Director: It's an association of those who speak many tongues.

Professor: And do they learn these tongues when they're very young?

Director: Yes, and they shadow translators in their work until they can take on simple tasks on their own.

Professor: And then they graduate to higher level work, like diplomatic translation?

Director: Exactly.

Professor: But would you sacrifice the common tongue in order for this guild-like thing to exist?

Director: Why, no. The translators themselves would speak a common tongue. They would be the truly global class.

Professor: They would speak this among themselves and only themselves?

Director: Yes.

Professor: Would it be a difficult language?

Director: None more difficult. And it would constantly evolve.

Professor: You've certainly piqued my curiosity. So tell me why this class of translators would be good.

Director: Well, if we all have a common tongue, isn't it likely that some or many of the languages in the world might fall out of use and die?

Professor: There's a chance of that, over a long enough period of time.

Director: And if that happens, there's less diversity in the world because there are fewer languages spoken?

Professor: True.

Director: But there's a funny thing. On the way to this lesser amount of diversity, there will be more.

Professor: How?

Director: Speakers of non-common languages will have more diversity as they first learn the common.

Professor: Because they'll retain their original along with the new? But if the original dies out over generations, there's less diversity.

Director: Right. But if we have no generally spoken common tongue and employ a translator class?

Professor: We'll probably have more living languages in the world, and more diversity.

Director: Yes, but what happens with the individuals?

Professor: They likely have only their native tongue.

Director: So not much diversity with them?

Professor: Not much diversity with them.

Director: But we'll have great diversity in the translator class itself.

Professor: That's true.

Director: Possibly more diversity than ever before among any one group?

Professor: Yes. But maybe people can study languages with the translators?

Director: Who do you think would want to do that?

Professor: The curious, or those with an interest in another tongue.

Director: Curiosity I can understand. But what interest would someone have?

Professor: Oh, who can say? Maybe they fell in love with someone from another language group. Love motivates, you know.

Director: And if there were only one tongue?

Professor: That might take some of the charm out of this love. There's something intriguing in the foreign.

Director: Why?

Professor: Because otherness fires the imagination.

Director: And imagination enriches love?

Professor: Of course! But now I have to ask. Who will the translators love?

Director: Anyone they want.

Professor: Do you think it will usually be other translators?

Director: I don't know. Do you think it matters?

Professor: I guess it doesn't. But if it's not another translator, will they teach their love the translator tongue?

Director: Not unless their love becomes a translator, too.

Professor: With no exceptions?

Director: With no exceptions.

Professor: But why?

Director: Because this is a language you earn.

44. WISDOM (MUSICIAN)

Musician: How can I tell you if musicians can be wise, if I don't even know what wisdom is?

Director: You really don't know?

Musician: Honestly and truly.

Director: Can't we say wisdom is knowing what to do?

Musician: Sure, why not?

Director: Do musicians know what to do?

Musician: Some of them do, about certain things.

Director: Like when to play what note?

Musician: And when to stay silent, yes.

Director: And that's musical wisdom?

Musician: It is.

Director: See? You do know what wisdom is.

Musician: For music, sure. But what about the rest of life?

Director: What about it? Doesn't it amount to much the same thing?

Musician: When to speak, and when to hold your tongue?

Director: Don't you think that's true?

Musician: You know, I do. But I think it's much harder.

Director: Why? Because you don't always know the score?

Musician: Ha, ha. You mean score in a double sense. Score as in written music, and score as in the game.

Director: What game?

Musician: The game of life!

Director: Who plays this game?

Musician: We all do!

Director: And who wins?

Musician: Shouldn't we say it's the wise?

Director: I don't know. Like you, I don't know enough about wisdom to say.

Musician: Oh, come on. What do you think we need to know about the wise?

Director: How they know when to speak up.

Musician: They speak when their interests are at stake. How's that?

Director: That's fine. But how do they know their interests?

Musician: Well, that's the real question, isn't it?

Director: Do you think they learn them on their own, or does someone teach them?

Musician: Who can teach you your interests?

Director: Someone who knows you very well.

Musician: Can anyone ever know us as well as we know ourselves?

Director: Yes, and sometimes better.

Musician: So these are our teachers in life?

Director: The only true teachers there are. Or don't you agree?

Musician: What's their interest?

Director: You're wondering why they're interested in us?

Musician: Yes. Why?

Director: Because the good in them likes to see others succeed.

Musician: Is that wise?

Director: I think it is.

Musician: And what of those who don't like to see others succeed?

Director: The jealous?

Musician: Yes.

Director: They're wretched.

Musician: Why, because they don't know how to stop others' success?

Director: No, they have a pretty good idea of how to do that.

Musician: Then why are they wretched?

Director: Because their success is never sweet.

45. Health (Musician)

Musician: Did you know a piece of music can be healthy?

Director: I did not. How can it be?

Musician: By standing on its own.

Director: But doesn't all music have to stand on its own?

Musician: You should ask me first what it means for it to stand on its own.

Director: What does it mean?

Musician: It means, stripped of all context, the piece impresses you.

Director: Stripped of all context? All context?

Musician: Yes.

Director: How is that possible? Didn't we say music is an associative phenomenon? A social phenomenon? That it doesn't exist in a vacuum?

Musician: Yes, yes. And all of that is true. But this is the test. When you listen to
something in isolation, with absolutely no knowledge about who made

the music, when, or how — and with no one else listening with you to color your judgment — that's when you get a view of its health.

Director: And what does health look like?

Musician: Health makes a strong impression.

Director: Even if there's no common ground between musician and listener?

Musician: Oh, don't get hung up on what we said before. Isolation renders common ground irrelevant. It's just you and the music.

Director: But what if the music makes a strong impression on you but not on me? Healthy?

Musician: Healthy music makes a strong impression on most.

Director: Ah, democratic health. So let's say there's a strong impression. Does that mean the song gets stuck in the listener's head?

Musician: The song gets stuck in their soul.

Director: So we're not talking about catchy advertising tunes.

Musician: No, we're talking about something that moves you, that stirs you deeply.

Director: Stuck and stirring. And that's a healthy thing?

Musician: Stirred up souls are healthy, yes.

Director: If you were a teacher of music, would you try to stir your students' souls?

Musician: Absolutely!

Director: How would you do it?

Musician: I'd start the semester by giving them some powerful music, but with no background information, no context at all. No artist name, no song title, no country of origin, no date of recording, no genre — nothing.

Director: So they can focus completely on how the music affects their soul?

Musician: Exactly.

Director: And what do you expect from them?

Musician: An essay describing the music the best they can.

Director: And then at the end of the semester?

Musician: The same thing.

Director: What improvement will you be looking for?

Musician: Less 'this music sounds like so-and-so and such-and-such' and more 'this music does this, this music does that'.

Director: Beyond music, can we describe people this way, the latter way?

Musician: Certainly.

Director: Would you like to be described that way?

Musician: I would.

Director: Why?

Musician: Because then we're describing me as me.

Director: So you'd rather not be flattered by being compared with someone else?

Musician: It's not always flattery. And no, I'd rather not.

Director: Why not?

Musician: It would make me seem derivative.

Director: Not an original?

Musician: Right. Only originals stand on their own.

Director: And what about those who are influenced here and there?

Musician: Well, we all have influences.

Director: Does it matter if we make them known?

Musician: It's a problem if we don't.

Director: Why?

Musician: Because how can it be good to pretend — we did it all on our own?

46. Over-Education (Professor)

Professor: It's sad, but some of my graduate students can't find jobs when they finish their degrees.

Director: Why not?

Professor: The teaching field is full, so they have to look elsewhere.

Director: And why doesn't elsewhere work out?

Professor: Because the graduates are often seen as over-qualified.

Director: You mean, you don't need an advanced degree for the jobs they're seeking.

Professor: Right.

Director: But what harm is there in having too much education, if you're perfectly willing to do the job?

Professor: Employers think you won't be happy.

Director: And that's the employer's primary concern?

Professor: Ha, ha. No, they think that because you're unhappy you'll leave as soon as you can find another job.

Director: But isn't there another reason?

Professor: You mean, the employer might be intimidated? Yes, that sometimes happens. But mostly I think they worry such a highly educated person won't be subordinate enough.

Director: Do you ever have worries like this?

Professor: Me? Ha! Of course not! Why would I?

Director: Maybe you have a student from time to time who's better educated than you.

Professor: Someone who already has an advanced degree and seeks another? I would have much to learn from them. But there's a danger if they carry on collecting degrees.

Director: What danger?

Professor: They might spread themselves too thin.

Director: And if they do?

Professor: Then they have more surface than depth.

Director: And depth is good.

Professor: Of course it is! And, yes, we have to have some breadth. But we have to decide where to really dive in.

Director: As you dove in on language.

Professor: Precisely.

Director: But language is a very broad topic. Some might say none is broader.

Professor: Yes, yes. It's no doubt broad. But you have to find a specialty within.

Director: How do you do that?

Professor: I'll tell you how it was for me. I found a handful of books I loved. And I started teaching them. And I taught them again, and again, until I acquired quite a degree of depth.

Director: What did you do for breadth?

Professor: As I looked around, I discovered other books, books related to the ones I was teaching. And I got to know them. And I started teaching them along with the others.

Director: So you kept your initial depth, spread out, and acquired more depth there.

Professor: Yes, but not as much there as with the original.

Director: Why not?

Professor: You can't be deep in everything, Director.

Director: You're over-educated if you are? But what's wrong with having depth everywhere? If you can do it, why not?

Professor: Here's the thing. We can always go deeper. Say I have one subject and I go a hundred feet down. Then I branch out to four other subjects and dig my way down a hundred feet with each.

Director: So you have five subjects at a depth of one hundred.

Professor: Yes. But in the time it took to dig into the additional four, I could have gone down that much more in my original area.

Director: I'm not sure I understand. So let me make it more extreme for contrast. Are you over-educated if you go down ten thousand feet, and have no other areas of depth?

Professor: No.

Director: But you're over-educated if you take on a hundred areas and dig to a hundred in each?

Professor: Yes and no. You're over-educated in the sense of trying to take on too much. But you're under-educated in not deepening your original area of expertise.

Director: But is it enough to deepen your expertise? Didn't you say we need some breadth?

Professor: Of course we do! Spread out all you like. Just don't neglect your original.

Director: What happens when you neglect your original?

Professor: You're lost.

Director: Lost in the breadth?

Professor: Yes. You have to get back home.

Director: And dig, and dig, and dig?

Professor: The metaphor is wearing thin.

Director: What's wrong with digging?

Professor: When you dig you're left with nothing but a hole.

Director: But what if you strike diamonds or gold?

Professor: We're not in the mining business, Director. Though it's good to un-earth new facts.

Director: What business are we in?

Professor: You know what business we're in.

Director: And in this business, the deeper we go, the more understanding we have?

Professor: Yes. And some resent this, you know.

Director: Who would resent such a thing?

Professor: The shallow.

Director: Why?

Professor: Because the deep awaken an old suspicion.

Director: What suspicion?

Professor: That the shallow should have gone deep, while they still had the chance.

47. The Streets (Musician)

Musician: Do you know what I never want educated out of me?

Director: Your common sense?

Musician: Close. My street-smarts.

Director: Street-smarts? What does that mean?

Musician: You know what it means.

Director: You know your way around your leafy suburban neighborhood?

Musician: Ha, ha. No, it means I know my way around the city.

Director: And your education might make you lose your way?

Musician: Formal education can blind you.

Director: How can it do that?

Musician: By giving you an artificial view of the world.

Director: Which world?

Musician: Ha, ha. My point exactly.

Director: So you're saying you need a natural view in order to find your way?

Musician: Yes.

Director: Do formal and artificial necessarily go hand in hand?

Musician: Not necessarily. But they often stick together.

Director: Why do you think that is?

Musician: I blame both teachers and students.

Director: What's to blame?

Musician: Many of them are looking for an escape from the streets.

Director: Why would they want that? Don't they want to know their way?

Musician: They don't want the world to be that way.

Director: What way?

Musician: Tough, and complicated, and seductive, and dangerous, and thrilling.

Director: So they want their school to be free of this? But what about you? Do you like it that way?

Musician: It doesn't matter if I do. It's the way it is.

Director: Yes, but you could choose to travel different streets. You could be suburb-smart, or university-smart.

Musician: Oh, forget about suburb-smart. What would it mean to be university-smart?

Director: To be wise to the university's ways.

Musician: Like the way it violates its trust with truth?

Director: What do you mean?

Musician: It lies about the outside world.

Director: It lies? Or has it lost touch?

Musician: What difference does it make? The university claims to teach about the world. Either way, the claim is false.

Director: Where does the falsehood slip in?

Musician: Where professors who've never seen the streets teach as though they had.

Director: That counts you out for teaching, then?

Musician: Ha, ha.

Director: But surely some professors have seen the streets.

Musician: You can see but not really see.

Director: I see. So maybe professors should only teach about the inside world.

Musician: What do you mean?

Director: They might teach the history of the university, and all it has done and been.

Musician: But even then, it has to see itself in context. And for that it needs truth about the outside world.

Director: Then why don't people like you teach professors to put their work in context this way?

Musician: I think we should. But there's a problem.

Director: Oh?

Musician: No one will listen.

Director: Why not?

Musician: Most believe their work is in context already.

Director: And the rest?

Musician: They don't think that's what universities are for.

48. FORTRESSES (PROFESSOR)

Professor: But the university already has too much of the outside world in it!

Director: It should be a fortress?

Professor: Yes.

Director: Why?

Professor: The students need a safe place in which to develop.

Director: Develop into what?

Professor: Fully educated human beings.

Director: Those who know and understand?

Professor: Precisely.

Director: But there are many outside the university who know and understand.

Professor: Yes, but what do they know and understand?

Director: What are you suggesting?

Professor: Successful students climb up and grasp the highest things.

Director: Why can't those on the outside do the same?

Professor: They can, but it's harder when you do it on your own.

Director: So, say I want to climb up and grasp the highest things concerning six-teenth century fashion trends. It's easier to do that in a university?

Professor: Oh, you're trying to trivialize things. But the answer is yes. And fashion can be important, you know. It tells us a lot about the way a people thinks of itself.

Director: So we can learn some psychology from fashion?

Professor: Yes. And we can learn some economics, too. After all, someone has to pay for the clothes.

Director: And with economics we get a window into politics, I suppose.

Professor: Yes. And so on, and so on. So do you see how it's easier to learn all this in a university than outside on your own?

Director: I take your point. But I still don't understand why the university needs to be a fortress.

Professor: The fortress keeps out distractions.

Director: Distractions that might cause a student to fall while climbing?

Professor: Yes.

Director: What kind of distractions?

Professor: We protect our students from those who would halt their climb.

Director: Why would anyone halt their climb?

Professor: You act as if you've never heard of such a thing!

Director: Oh, I've heard of it. But I want to know why it's done.

Professor: Do you want the basic reason or an elaborate theory?

Director: The basic will do.

Professor: Then know this. People who attempt to halt a climb, do so from envy and hate.

49. High and Low (Musician)

Director: Tell me, Musician. Is music highbrow or low?

Musician: It depends on the music. But I don't like those terms.

Director: Why not?

Musician: Professor told me where they come from. Have you heard of phrenology?

Director: The study of the shape and size of the cranium?

Musician: Yes, in order to tell things about a person's intellect and character. Don't you think it sounds awful?

Director: It certainly does. And I hear more things of this sort are in the works.

Musician: That's the last thing we need.

Director: Yes. Then maybe we shouldn't use these terms in describing music. Maybe we should just say whether it's high or low, forgetting about the brow.

Musician: That seems best.

Director: So tell me what your music is.

Musician: It's both high and low.

Director: Is being both superior to being one or the other?

Musician: It's better than being just low.

Director: And what about being just high?

Musician: You really can't say that's best these days.

Director: Why not?

Musician: Because you'll seem elitist.

Director: But high doesn't mean elite.

Musician: What does it mean?

Director: The high causes you to look up, above yourself.

Musician: It inspires?

Director: Yes.

Musician: I like that idea. It creates a longing.

Director: Longing?

Musician: To be the best you can be!

Director: Yes, but you need to tell your fans to exercise care.

Musician: Why?

Director: Don't you know the story of the philosopher who looked to the heavens as he went on his way?

Musician: No, what story?

Director: It's short. I'll tell it to you now.

Musician: Good! I love stories.

Director: Well, here it is. He kept looking up... and fell in a hole.

Musician: Ha! Then I'll have to tell my fans to stop before they look up.

Director: Stop, look up, look level, proceed. Is that how it goes?

Musician: That's how it goes. And now I have the seed for a song!

Director: That's good. But it's really too bad.

Musician: What's too bad?

Director: That our philosopher friend never climbed out of his hole.

Musician: Oh. I never thought to ask. It is too bad. He could have helped me with my tune.

50. Ideas (Musician)

Director: Are ideas real?

Musician: I can't believe you're asking! Of course they're real.

Director: Where do they come from?

Musician: Two places. We come up with them on our own. Or we get them from others.

Director: When they come from others, how do they come?

Musician: What do you mean? People share their ideas.

Director: And if they don't, can we pick them up indirectly?

Musician: Without being told? Yes, but I think that falls more into the category of coming up with them on our own.

Director: So they're either explained to us or we figure them out ourselves?

Musician: Right.

Director: What explaining do you do, Musician?

Musician: Me?

Director: Don't you explain musical ideas?

Musician: Ha! I do it all the time.

Director: How do you do it?

Musician: I do it in my songs!

Director: Yes, but how?

Musician: I establish a theme and then I run through the variations.

Director: The variations help explain the theme?

Musician: Yes, they do. They let you see the theme in a different light, from various perspectives.

Director: But not from all perspectives?

Musician: Well, that's the thing. The audience might only enjoy certain perspectives. So it's a judgment call for the artist.

Director: Does this hold for non-musical ideas?

Musician: What do you mean?

Director: Can we say that explaining those ideas is like writing music?

Musician: Sure we can. And I think what we said about perspective applies here, as well.

Director: Now, you specialize in a certain sort of popular music. Yes?

Musician: I do.

Director: Should those who explain non-musical ideas specialize, too?

Musician: I think they have to.

Director: Why?

Musician: There are so many ideas in the world!

Director: How does someone choose a specialty?

Musician: They find what fits.

Director: Fits?

Musician: Fits them.

Director: How do you know what fits?

Musician: You do what every good artist does. You experiment.

Director: And then you judge what suits you?

Musician: Right.

Director: What happens if an artist judges poorly?

Musician: The audience will react in a bad way.

Director: The audience doesn't like it if you're not properly suited for what you perform?

Musician: Of course it doesn't.

Director: Even if you have a great deal of talent?

Musician: Even then.

Director: Is fit more important than talent?

Musician: I wouldn't say that. I'd say fit is the base on which your talent stands.

Director: And it's ideas that fit. So we stand on our ideas?

Musician: Absolutely. And don't mind the switch in metaphor.

Director: I won't. It somehow seems appropriate. But tell me. What if we feel a need to examine our ideas more closely?

Musician: You mean we haven't explored all the perspectives? That's simple. We get out of the limelight, climb down, and see what we need to see.

Director: How willing are most to get out of the limelight?

Musician: Ha! Not very.

Director: What would make them?

Musician: If they start to feel mush beneath their feet.

Director: Because their ideas are rotten?

Musician: Yes. Then they're forced to get down.

Director: And when they have?

Musician: They search for replacements.

Director: And if they find them? If their platform again seems firm?

Musician: They climb right up, and start all over again.

51. Qualifications (Professor)

Professor: Yes, Director, we want our incoming students not to have heads like stones.

Director: But how can you be sure they don't?

Professor: The easiest way is through our interview process. We bring up ideas and see what they have to say.

Director: Well, I'm relieved. But what about the qualifications for professors? Do you have interviews for them?

Professor: Yes, of course.

Director: And what do you hope to learn?

Professor: That the candidates have a lively appreciation of ideas.

Director: I like to think I have a lively appreciation of ideas. Can I come and teach biochemistry?

Professor: Ha, ha. You need an advanced degree in the field.

Director: So, an advanced degree and a certain liveliness. What else?

Professor: The dreaded publications.

Director: Why are they dreaded? Don't you people like to write?

Professor: Yes, many do. But what I dread is reading certain academics.

Director: Why? Are they stifling?

Professor: Yes. Unless....

Director: Unless what?

Professor: Unless you get into the game of politics. Then you read with a sharp eye, looking to boost or attack.

Director: Are you in the game?

Professor: No longer, no. I tired of it.

Director: But you write books.

Professor: Yes, I do.

Director: Are they addressed to academics?

Professor: I'm afraid they are. But they're no longer bold, and don't provoke much of a response.

Director: Why do you write them?

Professor: Because my students sometimes read them.

Director: How does that make you feel?

Professor: Hopeful.

Director: Why hopeful?

Professor: Because then I feel all my effort hasn't been for nothing.

Director: Why don't you leave the academy, Professor?

Professor: Ha, ha.

Director: You could write books from outside.

Professor: I know you're trying to help, Director. But I don't believe I'm qualified for that.

Director: Why not?

Professor: Because all my experience is academic.

Director: Then take a sabbatical and acquire some non-academic skills.

Professor: Well, I would be more fresh after that.

Director: And good teachers are fresh. So will you do it?

Professor: I promise I'll look into it.

Director: Good. So what's the first non-academic skill you'll seek?

Professor: A flair for the popular in my writing.

Director: How will you achieve that?

Professor: I'll read a great deal of popular books.

Director: And with time, will the popular taste become your own?

Professor: Ha, ha. I have a taste for that already. Don't you know many of the classics are popular to the highest degree?

Director: Then why not start writing now?

Professor: Because most of my life I've been writing from a particular point of view.

Director: What point of view?

Professor: That of a critic.

Director: And this no longer appeals?

Professor: It never appealed.

Director: Then why did you write that way, the critics' way?

Professor: Because I didn't trust enough in my own.

52. FRIENDS (PROFESSOR)

Professor: I don't have many friends at the university.

Director: Why not?

Professor: I spend all my time on my students. And when I'm not with them, I research and write.

Director: Do you enjoy your students?

Professor: Very much so.

Director: But you don't think of them as your friends.

Professor: Why, no. I'm the professor.

Director: What about former students?

Professor: Off they go to their busy lives. Sure, I get notes from them, time to time. But that's about it.

Director: Do you want more friends?

Professor: I'd like more readers.

Director: I thought you don't like what you write.

Professor: Yes, but I intend to change.

Director: So the reader will be your friend?

Professor: The reader will be my greatest friend! No offense meant.

Director: None taken. But why will the reader be such a good friend?

Professor: Because with them I can share, and share, and share.

Director: And they always understand?

Professor: No, not always. But often enough? Yes.

Director: I don't know, Professor.

Professor: What don't you know?

Director: How often is enough.

Professor: Look. Do people completely understand you in your day-to-day life?

Director: Of course not.

Professor: How many would have to understand for you to say it's enough?

Director: It's never enough. I always hope for greater understanding, if understanding is the right word.

Professor: What other word would it be?

Director: Well, I might want people to know me. Or should I say I want them to feel me? And maybe I just want some appreciation.

Professor: Ah, appreciation. I'd rather have that.

Director: Why?

Professor: Because appreciation is the best of all.

Director: How so?

Professor: Think, for example, of a fool. You can know the fool. You can understand the fool. You might even feel the fool. But that doesn't mean you appreciate this fool.

Director: Appreciation involves admiration?

Professor: Yes, that puts it well. In fact, I'd say to appreciate is to admire.

Director: I thought to appreciate means to recognize someone's full worth. So, in that sense, I might appreciate a fool, their worth perhaps being small.

Professor: Alright, alright. We're not here to argue definitions.

Director: Yes, we're here to talk about the reader, our friend. How can we know a given reader is our friend?

Professor: Why would you ask that?

Director: Doesn't your experience in academic politics make you wonder?

Professor: Well, yes. It does. Some readers will be out to get us.

Director: They'll try to make us look bad?

Professor: Of course.

Director: What can we do? What do you do?

Professor: I consider the source.

Director: The wretched will have wretched things to say?

Professor: Always.

Director: And the good will have good things to say?

Professor: Provided our work is good.

Director: So we need good work. How will we get it?

Professor: We must commune within.

Director: And that's how you write?

Professor: It is.

Director: But what about our friend, the reader?

Professor: What about them?

Director: Do they really want some solipsistic soliloquy? Isn't giving them that a bit... arrogant?

Professor: Yes, but how else can we write?

Director: With one eye on ourselves, and the other on the reader.

Professor: But then that begs the question — which reader? Do you believe in a special reader, a sort of guiding star?

Director: Actually, I'd rely on several such stars.

Professor: And are these stars real or ideal?

Director: They're ideal in that they're real.

Professor: Ha. And what makes someone a star for you?

Director: That they are or had been a friend.

53. LOVE (MUSICIAN)

Director: I wonder if what I've heard is true.

Musician: What have you heard?

Director: That all musicians are lovers.

Musician: Ha! Of course it's not true.

Director: Why do you sound so certain?

Musician: Because you can write a love song with a cold heart.

Director: How do you know that?

Musician: I have inside information.

Director: But can you perform a love song with a cold heart?

Musician: No doubt. Performers who seem passionate sometimes only seem.

Director: They might be actors in addition to musicians?

Musician: Exactly. Haven't you ever heard a band referred to as an act?

Director: I have. And you're really introducing me to the mysteries now.

Musician: There's really not much mystery here. Not everyone is authentic.

Director: I always wonder about that word. Authentic. What does it mean? No acting? Or does it mean you believe your own act?

Musician: Ha, ha. But what about you? Are you a lover?

Director: That question's unfair. We're talking about musicians. And I make no claim to music. So what about you?

Musician: Am I a lover when I write? I suppose I am. I only write when I'm in the mood.

Director: Are you often in the mood?

Musician: The mood for love? I am.

Director: So you often write songs of love. But what about when you perform? Are you always in the mood?

Musician: Of course not. But, as they say, the show must go on.

Director: Why must it go on?

Musician: Because people paid to see it.

Director: Are you really that cynical?

Musician: Ha, ha! No, I'm not. I believe a bond forms between good musicians and the audience. The show must go on out of respect for the bond.

Director: Now what about the university?

Musician: What about it?

Director: Can it teach you love?

Musician: Not unless I fall in love with one of my professors! But, really, who can teach love? You experience love and learn what you can.

Director: And you write what you learn?

Musician: That's what lyricists do.

Director: Do you need certain language skills to write about love?

Musician: You need certain basic tools.

Director: Yes, but the better equipped you are the more nuance you must be able to catch. Isn't that why you're studying here?

Musician: Yes, but sometimes simple is best.

Director: I agree. Now in addition to language, you study music. How do the professors teach the tools for depicting love?

Musician: It doesn't really work like that.

Director: What do you mean?

Musician: I mean, they don't have a course called 'The Musical Tools for Love'.

Director: Should they?

Musician: I don't know. They have songwriting courses.

Director: Where they teach the rudimentary and even advanced compositional skills?

Musician: Yes, of course. Mostly the advanced. They expect you to know the basics.

Director: And love is a very basic thing.

Musician: True. But sometimes it warrants the most advanced tools we can muster.

Director: But if you don't know love in its basic form, what do all your fancy tools matter?

Musician: Director, I'm on your side.

Director: Then do you agree to this? No matter what you learn from others, the essence of love in a song is up to you.

Musician: Of course!

Director: Yes. But I worry for you.

Musician: Why?

Director: I don't know if you're properly prepared to write about love.

Musician: You're ridiculous! But tell me how I can be properly prepared.

Director: You need more practice.

Musician: Musical practice?

Director: Why, no. Practice in love.

54. Religion (Professor)

Professor: We no longer offer religious education at our university.

Director: So there's a vacuum?

Professor: Not quite. We teach religious studies.

Director: Why?

Professor: What do you mean, 'Why?'

Director: What do people hope to learn from studying various religions? How to make a better one, or how to make one better?

Professor: Ha, ha. To be honest, I don't know what they hope to learn. But I know one thing. It's not meant to be an exercise in comparison shopping.

Director: Intent and effect often differ.

Professor: What do you think is the intent of these courses?

Director: I think the professors teaching them would say religion is a fundamental part of humanity. And all things human should interest us.

Professor: That's probably the strongest reason they can give. But it's religion at a remove.

Director: True. But that makes me wonder. Doesn't your university teach religion at no remove?

Professor: Director, I just said it doesn't.

Director: Yes, but maybe it's not aware it does.

Professor: Ha! So where do we look to find this religion?

Director: A good place to start is with what the university believes.

Professor: What does the university believe?

Director: Shouldn't you tell me?

Professor: Ha, ha. Okay. The university believes in education.

Director: Has education become a religion?

Professor: Maybe in a sense. But the university believes in more.

Director: What does the university believe?

Professor: It believes in equality.

Director: All are equally entitled to an education, if they meet the standards for admission?

Professor: Exactly. And it goes much further.

Director: How so?

Professor: Equality permeates all of education, as a principle.

Director: So is belief in education and equality enough for a religion?

Professor: No, I think it takes more.

Director: What more?

Professor: The university believes in merit.

Director: What does that mean?

Professor: The university is a meritocracy where excellence finds reward.

Director: Don't you mean where following the professor finds reward?

Professor: Ha, ha. That sort of thing happens, mostly in the arts. But it does happen in the sciences, in less obvious ways. Still, excellence always stands out.

Director: And does it always have its reward?

Professor: That's a big question, Director.

Director: Is it a question of justice?

Professor: Of course.

Director: If you're going to believe in a religion, does it have to be just?

Professor: No one believes in an unjust religion.

Director: Some of the ancients did.

Professor: Well, you may have a point.

Director: Now what about with the other two beliefs?

Professor: Are there questions of justice with them? Well, it's unjust if you're not equal.

Director: And with the belief in education?

Professor: I'm not sure how there's justice in that.

Director: Wouldn't you say education is supposed to be useful? Wouldn't you say it's supposed to make you better?

Professor: Yes, certainly.

Director: If your education somehow makes you worse, wouldn't that be unjust?

Professor: I think it would.

Director: How can education make you worse?

Professor: I don't know.

Director: Then maybe we should say how it makes you better. How do you make your students better, Professor?

Professor: I help them obtain knowledge concerning language.

Director: So knowledge makes them better? Can we apply this to all fields of study?

Professor: Yes, I think that's fair to say.

Director: What's the opposite of knowledge?

Professor: Ignorance.

Director: Ignorance makes us worse?

Professor: If we started out with knowledge, it does.

Director: But if we come to the university with ignorance, and we leave with ignorance, we're neither better nor worse?

Professor: Yes. But that means the university has failed.

Director: So what does this have to do with religion?

Professor: Ha! You should tell me!

Director: It's rather simple. If the university makes you better, you'll likely believe in it and what it does.

Professor: And if it doesn't make you better?

Director: You'll look elsewhere for your faith.

55. Power (Professor)

Director: I know there are academic politics. But does the university as a whole play politics with the outside world?

Professor: Well, like any large institution, the university gets embroiled in politics from time to time.

Director: Yes, but playing and being embroiled are two different things.

Professor: What do you think makes for the difference?

Director: Would you rather play or be embroiled?

Professor: I'd rather play.

Director: That's the difference.

Professor: Ha, ha. Yes, it's true.

Director: When the university plays politics, what are its terms?

Professor: Well, look at it this way. What does the university do?

Director: It educates.

Professor: Of course. But how does the university educate?

Director: In a certain way?

Professor: Yes, yes. But what does that certain way have to do with?

Director: Beliefs about justice?

Professor: Yes! And what happens when many are properly educated in beliefs about justice?

Director: Good things happen?

Professor: Ha, ha! Yes, good things! And who will make these things happen?

Director: Future political actors educated by your school.

Professor: Right. So do you see how the university plays politics?

Director: It takes a long view.

Professor: Exactly.

Director: So tell me what's better, in the long view. University trained political actors with little power, or university trained political actors with lots of power?

Professor: Oh, don't be so crude.

Director: Sorry. But what's the answer?

Professor: You know the answer.

Director: And what about those who aren't university trained?

Professor: What about them?

Director: Are they the enemy?

Professor: Of course not! Not unless their standards of justice differ, that is.

Director: They can come to the university's standards on their own?

Professor: Director, these are universal standards.

Director: Then why do we need the university?

Professor: It's easier when you're properly trained.

Director: What's hard about justice?

Professor: Justice is embattled in this world. Some people believe in and live what's right. Others don't.

Director: And these others are powerful?

Professor: In a vulgar sort of way, they are.

Director: Power can be vulgar? Or do you mean the use of power can be vulgar?

Professor: The use of power.

Director: And the university teaches the opposite of this?

Professor: The opposite of vulgar use? Yes, of course.

Director: What's the opposite of vulgarity?

Professor: Sophistication.

Director: And?

Professor: I'm not sure what you're looking for.

Director: Could it be good taste? Or have I got it wrong?

Professor: No, you've got it right. Good taste and sophistication are the opposites of vulgarity.

Director: And you teach these things.

Professor: We certainly do.

Director: I can imagine how you teach sophistication. You familiarize the students with the complexities of power and its use. But how do you teach good taste?

Professor: We teach them good aesthetic judgment.

Director: Judgment concerning beauty?

Professor: Yes, of course.

Director: Is power beautiful?

Professor: Well....

Director: How about justice?

Professor: You know it is.

Director: Then does this follow?

Professor: What?

Director: If the university offers a political education, an education in justice, it also offers an education in beauty. No?

Professor: I'm not sure that necessarily follows. But in the case of our school, it's true. Our students learn the beauty.

Director: And when they have?

Professor: Justice is much less an abstraction to them.

Director: What does that mean?

Professor: It means we make justice vibrant and real.

Director: Yes, but how?

Professor: By using every bit of power we have — to put it into effect.

56. Meaning 3 (Professor)

Director: What are the limits of education?

Professor: Why do you ask?

Director: Because certain educators seem to think the sky's the limit. Is it?

Professor: It depends on the student.

Director: What student has the sky as their limit?

Professor: Someone who's willing to learn.

Director: That's it? That's all it takes?

Professor: Well, honestly? It takes a great deal of talent, too.

Director: But even talent has its limits, no?

Professor: True. But talent is less limited when exercised properly.

Director: Then proper exercise is very important. What is the proper?

Professor: Someone could get an advanced degree in answering that question.

Director: Yes, but let's have a simple definition.

Professor: I don't have one to offer.

Director: You, a professor of language, don't know this simple word?

Professor: I don't claim to know everything.

Director: Yes, but you used the word. Don't you know the rule? Never use a word unless you're sure of its meaning.

Professor: Ha, ha. If I followed that, I'd hardly speak!

Director: Is that an occupational hazard?

Professor: Being uncertain of words? Yes, it is. If you look too closely at anything, you'll see it's not that simple. And I look very, very closely at words.

Director: Do you think you shouldn't?

Professor: Ha, ha! No! And you just used a word I'm not so sure of. Shouldn't.

Director: I'll hazard a definition for you. 'Shouldn't' means it's advisable not to do what others don't expect.

Professor: What? Ha! That's an awful definition in so many ways!

Director: How so?

Professor: For one, what if they don't expect you to do something good?

Director: Ah, you've found a weakness. How can we improve the definition?

Professor: We'll put it in a positive light. How's this? 'Should' encourages you to do what's best.

Director: Now I see why you're the professor, not me.

Professor: Ha, ha. But let's explore your definition a bit. Who are the others you mentioned? And what do they expect?

Director: Who are they? People who do what they should. And what do they expect? Words to have stable meanings.

Professor: What did you say?

Director: People who do —

Professor: No, not that.

Director: Stable meanings for words?

Professor: Yes. Don't you think we all expect that?

Director: Even lovers of words?

Professor: Ha! You see right through me.

Director: What's the limit with lovers?

Professor: What do you mean?

Director: I mean, how far are the lovers willing to go with less than stable words?

Professor: As far as there's pleasure in them.

Director: And what about stability itself?

Professor: What about it?

Director: What does it mean?

Professor: You should tell me.

Director: Alright. Stability means a word's meaning is shared and clear to all.

Professor: Ha! Then no word ever has been or will be stable!

Director: Not even the words no and yes?

Professor: You'll have to read a book I have on the meanings of those words.

Director: Is this the sort of thing you teach?

Professor: It is, and I love it.

Director: Tell me more about your love.

Professor: I love to influence the odds.

Director: I don't understand.

Professor: Let me explain. If there are one hundred people, and ninety understand a word to mean one thing, while ten understand it to mean another — I want to side with the ten, and change the odds.

Director: Are you saying meaning is about probability, or something like that?

Professor: Yes! And that's a wonderful insight.

Director: Will you give me an honorary degree for it?

Professor: Keep it up, Director, and the sky will be the limit for you!

Director: Thanks. But now I'm wondering about stability.

Professor: What are you wondering?

Director: I said, 'Stability means a word's meaning is shared and clear to all.' But we didn't limit that 'all'.

Professor: You mean, we assumed all meant everyone.

Director: Yes. But it could have meant, for instance, all my friends, or all who know.

Professor: Ah, Director. If you start trying to speak the unspoken you're in for quite a time.

Director: Why do you say that?

Professor: Because you're going to have to limit the limits! You'll have to limit, for instance, your use of 'friend'.

Director: Well, it's a wonder people communicate at all. So it's good not to look too closely at these things?

Professor: Oh, I'm not saying that.

Director: What are you saying?

Professor: If you're someone who can't resist taking a closer look, just be prepared — to see what you'd never expect.

57. APTITUDE (MUSICIAN)

Director: Are all students created equal?

Musician: Of course not.

Director: In what sense aren't they?

Musician: In terms of aptitude.

Director: What is aptitude?

Musician: It's a natural ability to do something.

Director: But can't a student learn how to do something even if not naturally gifted?

Musician: Of course. But the one with a natural aptitude will also be learning.

Director: Learning how to get better?

Musician: Yes.

Director: And so while we all can learn, some of us go further.

Musician: Right. So the trick is finding what your aptitude is.

Director: We all have an aptitude for something?

Musician: Do you think some of us have an aptitude for nothing?

Director: Literally nothing? That seems hard to believe. But if you don't find your aptitude, I suppose it feels that way.

Musician: Yes, I think it does. But listen to us! We're talking as if people only have an aptitude for one thing, when we know full well some people have an aptitude for many.

Director: Tell me, Musician. Would you rather have one aptitude or many?

Musician: Many, of course.

Director: But what if the one thing is much more valuable than the many others combined?

Musician: Well, is the one thing's value conventional or otherwise?

Director: That's a good question. Which would you prefer?

Musician: I prefer the latter.

Director: Why?

Musician: Ha! Why? Because conventional value varies!

Director: You mean, for the first half of your life, for instance, your aptitude is highly valued, and then things change?

Musician: Yes, in the second half of your life your aptitude isn't valued at all.

Director: I think we need an example.

Musician: Okay. Here's an extreme one. Suppose you live in a tyranny, and you have an aptitude for taking direction in order to write propaganda.

Director: So you have two aptitudes? Taking direction and writing propaganda?

Musician: Yes. But what happens if on your fortieth birthday the tyrant falls?

Director: You're suggesting the value of propaganda falls, too?

Musician: I am. And doesn't it?

Director: Almost certainly. But surely writing skills are valued in the new state.

Musician: True, but it's not the same thing.

Director: And what about taking direction?

Musician: What about it?

Director: The new state doesn't value that as much?

Musician: Of course it doesn't, not like a tyranny. But let's say something about value that never changes. Can you think of an example?

Director: How about defending yourself?

Musician: Yes, that always has value, great value. But only some of us have natural ability here.

Director: Why do you say that?

Musician: You don't think some people have a very hard time defending themselves?

Director: I'm sure they do. But do they lack the aptitude? Or is it something else?

Musician: What else do you have in mind?

Director: A reason.

Musician: A reason? They lack a reason to defend themselves?

Director: Sometimes. And sometimes they have a reason but fail to give it adequate support.

Musician: Why do you think that is?

Director: They don't value themselves enough.

Musician: No, I don't think that's why.

Director: Then why?

Musician: They're just not brave.

58. Resistance (Musician)

Musician: Some people resist most things as a matter of principle.

Director: Why?

Musician: Because they can't always tell what truly needs resisting, and they don't want to take a chance.

Director: So what happens if they resist something good?

Musician: They hope it will keep on coming back.

Director: Until they learn to see?

Musician: Yes, until they see it for what it is.

Director: But what if they learn too late?

Musician: Then they hope there will be other good things like this they'll recognize right away.

Director: Their principle involves a lot of hope.

Musician: Well, consider the opposite principle. You let most things in. Doesn't that, too, involve a great deal of hope?

Director: You have a point. You hope good things come in, and the bad doesn't find its way to your door.

Musician: So which hope do you prefer?

Director: I prefer to build a receiving room where I can greet all who come.

Musician: And if you like them, you let them in the rest of the house?

Director: Yes. But we spend as long in the receiving room as I like or need. What do you think?

Musician: I think some would still resist, resist letting them further in.

Director: That's fine, so long as they take the time to talk.

Musician: But we can be fooled by talk, and the music of talk.

Director: Ah, the music. But are you, a musician, troubled by this?

Musician: Of course I am. You can't just listen to the words. You have to listen to how the words are said. And if they're said in a beautiful way....

Director: You're susceptible to beauty.

Musician: I have a weakness for beauty, yes.

Director: And so whatever your resistance, it's primarily aimed at that?

Musician: It is.

Director: Well, this changes everything.

Musician: How so?

Director: You're worried a beautiful act might take you in.

Musician: Everyone should worry about that.

Director: But I don't think general resistance is a good idea. We should be open to beauty.

Musician: So what should we do?

Director: Listen first for beauty in the words themselves. Then listen for tone.

Musician: And if they match?

Director: There might be integrity.

Musician: Or the person might be a very good actor.

Director: Then engage in dialogue and see if they hold up.

Musician: But isn't that a sort of resistance?

Director: Sure. But I'd liken it more to play. So play until you're all tired out, and see what you see.

Musician: But what will we talk about?

Director: Whatever you like, so long as you pay attention to just one thing.

Musician: What thing?

Director: Your comfort.

Musician: Ha! Comfort tells us it's safe to let them in?

Director: Comfort, yes. But comfort based on reason. You've been reasoning all this time.

Musician: Are you saying we always let in those who reason well?

Director: Well, it's not that simple. They have to be open to reason, too.

Musician: And then we know they're safe?

Director: If you can reason with them? The odds are better, yes.

Musician: Better isn't the same as good, Director.

Director: What can I say?

Musician: What would make the odds good?

Director: Evidence they never use reason in a particular way.

Musician: What way?

Director: For personal attacks.

Musician: Well, of course. But what about impersonal attacks?

Director: Attacks on your ideas? Yes, you should welcome them.

Musician: Ha! That's who I want in? Those who attack my ideas?

Director: You don't think your ideas can stand up to attack?

Musician: No, I know they can.

Director: How?

Musician: They've been attacked before.

Director: How do you know they stood up well?

Musician: How? Because I still believe in them!

Director: Then it seems you have nothing to fear.

Musician: Yes, but who wants their ideas attacked in their own home?

Director: Maybe we need to clarify something about attack.

Musician: What's to clarify?

Director: An attack can be gentle, you know.

Musician: Then why call it attack?

Director: Maybe we shouldn't.

Musician: So what would you call it?

Director: Something that makes you think.

59. Resistance 2 (Professor)

Professor: Yes, yes. But what does resistance have to do with education?

Director: There's nothing more important to learn.

Professor: And you think we can teach this at the university?

Director: I do, starting with you and your courses.

Professor: Why with me?

Director: Well, tell me. What must we resist?

Professor: Abuse.

Director: What kinds of abuse are there?

Professor: Physical and mental.

Director: With physical abuse, what's involved?

Professor: The body.

Director: And with mental abuse?

Professor: The mind.

Director: How do we access the mind?

Professor: Mostly? Through words.

Director: How do we resist an abusive word?

Professor: Also through words, I suppose.

Director: Now, you're an expert on words...

Professor: Ha, ha. So you assume I know how to resist?

Director: Maybe you just need reminding.

Professor: Then remind me how we resist mental abuse.

Director: We describe the abusers as they are.

Professor: In other words, we're honest.

Director: Yes. And we never cross the line into excess or abuse.

Professor: Because truth is the best resistance.

Director: Resistance to words, yes. So why don't you teach that?

Professor: But what's to teach? You speak truth or you don't.

Director: Yes, but there are many ways to speak truth. Haven't you heard of rhetoric?

Professor: Of course. But rhetoric is the skin we peel and throw away. Truth is the inner fruit.

Director: Do abusers deserve the inner truth?

Professor: About themselves? It's not a question of deserving.

Director: What's it a question of?

Professor: Effect.

60. Ease (Professor)

Director: Do students have to be at ease in order to learn?

Professor: It certainly helps.

Director: What do you do to set them at ease?

Professor: I try not to be intimidating.

Director: And how do you do that?

Professor: I'm gentle with them in the classroom. And I offer much time outside of class, for those who aren't comfortable in groups.

Director: Is discomfort the opposite of ease?

Professor: I think anxiety describes that opposite best.

Director: What might make a student anxious?

Professor: For some? Pressure to get good grades.

Director: Would it help if you promised everyone a good grade?

Professor: Ha, ha.

Director: Why do you think certain students care about grades?

Professor: They want to be able to get a good job.

Director: They want high paying jobs?

Professor: Not always. Some want to follow their passion into low paying work.

Director: But there's competition even for that?

Professor: Yes.

Director: Maybe that's the reason these students are anxious. Competition.

Professor: But they've been competing for grades their whole lives.

Director: Maybe some of them have been anxious their whole lives.

Professor: What do you think we can do about that?

Director: Eliminate the competition.

Professor: Ha! And how would we do that?

Director: Guarantee students jobs from the start.

Professor: How?

Director: Through a lottery.

Professor: Ha, ha! Now you're really being ridiculous.

Director: Oh, it wouldn't be completely random. We'd take students' interests into account.

Professor: But students discover their interests through their time in school!

Director: Then let the first two years be without grades, so they can freely explore. Then they'll put in their choices for the lottery.

Professor: I don't know, Director. Even if we could get employers to go along — which seems an insurmountable if — it doesn't seem fair.

Director: Is it more fair for those maniacally driven by ambition to get the best jobs?

Professor: Well.... What do you think really drives those people?

Director: I really think it's ambition.

Professor: Yes, but what about pressure from home?

Director: Could be. But won't home be happy with a guaranteed job?

Professor: Yes, but home might try to dictate the choices put into the lottery.

Director: Well, we can't fix everything.

Professor: Of course. But tell me, Director. How will this system help students who lack motivation?

Director: If they find a subject they enjoy during the exploratory years, I think they'll find their motivation.

Professor: And if they don't?

Director: As I said, we can't fix everything.

Professor: Let's get back to the maniacs. They have drive. And we want drive. Drive is good. But not drive like theirs. How do we distinguish the two?

Director: In other words, what makes a maniac?

Professor: That's what I want to know.

Director: I suppose it's single-mindedness.

Professor: Yes, I think there's something to that. How do we cure single-mindedness?

Director: We find the person another interest.

Professor: How do we do that?

Director: We have to encourage them to explore.

Professor: Yes, but how?

Director: Professor, isn't that the teacher's art?

Professor: Of course it is. Teachers use their influence to excite curiosity. But they don't have much sway with the single-minded.

Director: Then maybe we have to cut the single-minded off from their focus.

Professor: Ha! We might kill them if we do!

Director: So what can we do?

Professor: Take the longer view.

Director: What does that mean?

Professor: Accept the maniacs for what they are. But find a way to harness their drive.

Director: And if they learn they've been put into harness?

Professor: So long as they get a helping of praise and reward? I'm sure they won't mind a bit.

61. Fairness (Professor)

Professor: What do I hope my students will remember about me? That I was knowledgeable. That I was fair. That I cared.

Director: So it's one professional trait and two moral?

Professor: I suppose it is.

Director: Is that the right ratio?

Professor: Why, do you think it should be two professional and one moral?

Director: Let's explore a little and see. If you had to pick only one moral trait, what would it be?

Professor: Fairness.

Director: Is it possible you might be fair but really not care?

Professor: You mean I'm just going through the motions?

Director: Yes.

Professor: No, that's no good. My students would know.

Director: Know you don't care? But why does that matter if you're truly being fair?

Professor: Are you asking me seriously?

Director: Yes.

Professor: Knowing someone cares allows a bond to form.

Director: And you want to bond with your students.

Professor: Of course!

Director: Will professional traits help in forming this bond?

Professor: I think they should.

Director: Then let's turn to them now. The first trait is being knowledgeable. What's the second? You do agree there's more than knowledge, yes?

Professor: I do. The second is being very clear.

Director: You mean, being easily understood?

Professor: Well, I don't know. You might be clear about a very difficult subject, one that's not easily understood.

Director: Then how do we know if you're being clear?

Professor: I... don't know.

Director: Maybe you need someone competent to judge.

Professor: Someone who understands the difficult subject?

Director: Yes. Can't they tell if you're clear?

Professor: I suppose they can. But I want my students to know I'm clear.

Director: Then you want them to grasp the difficult subject, so they can know the truth about you.

Professor: Well, I want them to grasp it for more reason than that. But they'll have to strive in order to grasp.

Director: What's wrong with that?

Professor: What sustains them as they strive?

Director: Desire to know?

Professor: Yes, but there's more to it than that.

Director: What more?

Professor: They'll be sustained by taking me on trust.

Director: Trust that it's worth it to strive?

Professor: Yes.

Director: And how will you win their trust?

Professor: Through knowledge, clarity, fairness, and caring.

Director: What if you could do it with just the first three?

Professor: Impossible. Those three without caring are cold.

Director: And students mistrust the cold? Even if they find themselves in great heat as they strive?

Professor: Ha. Let's say you have a point. But let's move on.

Director: Alright. Here's something I wonder. Which is more clear? Specialized or everyday language?

Professor: It depends on how it's used.

Director: What would most specialists find more easy to use?

Professor: Most? The language of their specialty.

Director: Would it be hard for them to describe their subject in everyday words?

Professor: I think it would be very hard for some.

Director: And if they use jargon their audience doesn't know?

Professor: It would be hard on the audience.

Director: Are you hard on your students this way?

Professor: Of course not! I explain things in terms they can understand.

Director: You make it easy for them?

Professor: No, I wouldn't say that. They still have to work in order to know.

Director: And that's only fair?

Professor: Yes. Knowledge never comes cheap.

Director: But even so, you explain as much as you can?

Professor: Yes, I make things as clear as they can be.

Director: Is there anything you wouldn't explain in order to make things clear?

Professor: There's nothing I wouldn't explain.

Director: Because making things clear is effective?

Professor: Of course it is. And understanding is the effect.

Director: Is it the only effect?

Professor: Well, it's funny you should ask. There is another effect.

Director: What other effect do you want?

Professor: I want my students to know I didn't cheat.

Director: Cheat? How would you cheat?

Professor: I might try to seem more knowledgeable than I am.

Director: And you can't do that when you're clear?

Professor: Right.

Director: Why would anyone try to seem more knowledgeable than they are?

Professor: They want to enjoy more authority than they deserve. And that's un-fair.

Director: What do students learn from a teacher like this?

Professor: Nothing good, and many harmful things.

Director: What harmful things?

Professor: For one? The unfair teacher employs all sorts of tricks, subtle or not, to puff themselves up. And certain students emulate this.

Director: But aside from making them foolish, what's the harm?

Professor: The harm? Director, the habit of being unfair in one thing spills over into being unfair in all!

Director: Really? And what's the harm in being unfair?

Professor: Are you really asking me this?

Director: I am. I ask because I want to know, want to be sure.

Professor: Unfairness... amounts to harm!

Director: Hmm. If I'm good at soccer, and I don't get picked for the team, is that unfair?

Professor: Of course it is.

Director: Is it a harm?

Professor: Yes.

Director: But can't I shrug this harm off?

Professor: How?

Director: For instance? By taking up another sport instead. I won't allow myself to be harmed. Do you see what I'm saying?

Professor: Unfairness isn't harm unless we allow it to be? Maybe. Sometimes. But I think it takes a special sort of person for that.

Director: Why?

Professor: Because unfairness usually wins.

62. Boredom (Musician)

Musician: Nothing kills learning like boredom.

Director: You want your professors to entertain you?

Musician: No, I'm not saying that.

Director: What are you saying?

Musician: I want them to say something useful.

Director: Something that will help you get ahead?

Musician: No, not that, either. I want them to say something that will help me in life.

Director: I thought you were studying language with Professor. You wanted to improve your lyrics.

Musician: True.

Director: Have your lyrics improved?

Musician: They have.

Director: You use your lyrics for your music?

Musician: Of course.

Director: And your music is an important part of your life?

Musician: You know it is.

Director: Then Professor is helping you in life.

Musician: He is.

Director: Are you bored in Professor's class?

Musician: Never.

Director: So it's your other professors who bore you. Maybe you took the wrong courses.

Musician: I had no choice. They were required.

Director: How can we make required boredom interesting?

Musician: I wish I knew.

Director: Maybe you can ask polite but somewhat disruptive questions.

Musician: Ha, ha. Maybe I can.

Director: Would that make things interesting?

Musician: I think it might.

Director: Interesting for you or for the whole class?

Musician: For the whole class. And do you know why?

Director: Tell me.

Musician: The questions will tease out the knowledge we're not getting.

Director: Why, is the professor holding back?

Musician: Yes.

Director: But why would a professor hold back?

Musician: Because we want knowledge about the professor.

Director: You want the professors to talk about themselves?

Musician: Why not?

Director: But what if they're not very interesting?

Musician: That's an interesting fact to know.

Director: But once you know it, what then?

Musician: I'll ask about the elephant in the room.

Director: What elephant?

Musician: Boredom!

Director: What can you ask about that?

Musician: How what we're learning relates to life.

Director: No one is bored when they learn about life?

Musician: No one.

Director: Then why wouldn't all teachers talk about life?

Musician: That's what I want to know.

63. ANALYSIS (MUSICIAN)

Musician: Some seem to think memory is everything. But analysis is really what counts.

Director: Why?

Musician: Because you can remember everything in the world, but if you don't know what to make of it, what good does it do?

Director: To analyze is to make?

Musician: No, analysis breaks things down. But here's how it relates to making. If we're to build, we need parts. Good analysis breaks things down into usable parts.

Director: So the good analysis of a tree, for instance, results in lumber?

Musician: Metaphorically speaking? Yes.

Director: But the analysis might go further. It might break the tree down into molecules.

Musician: True.

Director: So we need to know when to stop?

Musician: Of course.

Director: But we also might get stuck along the way. If that happens, what can we do?

Musician: We can hire a psychologist.

Director: A psychologist can get us unstuck?

Musician: Yes, and a good one knows not to go too far once we're free.

Director: They don't worry us with molecules when what we need is lumber for a house.

Musician: Exactly.

Director: And if the psychologist isn't so good?

Musician: They dwell too long on things.

Director: What happens when they do?

Musician: We get too deep.

Director: And how do we know we're too deep?

Musician: We lose sight of the surface.

Director: The surface? What's the surface?

Musician: The only way out... or in.

64. ARGUMENT (PROFESSOR)

Director: When you teach language, do you teach argument?

Professor: Argument in the classical sense? A reasoned discussion aimed at persuading or being persuaded? Of course I do.

Director: Where do you begin?

Professor: Well, first of all, this is an advanced level course.

Director: Why should it be? Don't you want everyone to learn argument?

Professor: Yes, but you have to be prepared.

Director: How so?

Professor: You don't want to engage in reasoned argument unless you're ready to lose.

Director: Lose? Doesn't everyone in a reasoned argument win?

Professor: Ha, ha. Yes, of course. But not everyone sees it that way. They don't know it's not really losing to lose, if you know what I mean.

Director: But how else do you need to be prepared?

Professor: You have to be prepared to win.

Director: What does that involve?

Professor: Knowing that even though your side of the argument came out on top, it might be because the other didn't make their case as strong as it could be.

Director: Why might someone not make the best argument?

Professor: Because they're ignorant of what to say.

Director: Or because they're shy?

Professor: That could certainly be a reason.

Director: Shouldn't knowledge chase away shyness?

Professor: Shouldn't it? Of course it should! But does it?

Director: Tell me what you see in your classes.

Professor: Shy ones who've lost sometimes come to me in my office and discuss the argument. They make all sorts of wonderful points, points they didn't make in class while the argument was on.

Director: So knowledge didn't chase away shyness.

Professor: No.

Director: Why do you think that is?

Professor: Because people are afraid to win.

Director: Why are they afraid to win?

Professor: They don't want the attention.

Director: Why not?

Professor: Who can say? What makes someone shy?

Director: Maybe you can make that your class' next argument. And maybe you can ask two of the shy to make it.

Professor: Do you think they'll be more comfortable arguing shy to shy?

Director: I think there's a good chance, unless the attention of the rest of the class flusters them.

Professor: So what can we do about that?

Director: Ask them if they'd prefer to argue in semi-private.

Professor: Semi-private?

Director: In front of the two of us only.

Professor: Ha! You've invited yourself?

Director: What, did you think I was shy?

Professor: Ha, ha! No! But I think that's a great idea. We won't cheer the winner, and we won't put down the loser. This will be argument in the purest sense.

Director: And what do we hope to get from argument in the purest sense?

Professor: Beauty, and truth.

65. DOCILITY (PROFESSOR)

Director: What is docility?

Professor: Ha, ha. I wonder why you ask.

Director: Why do you think I ask?

Professor: Oh, I think it has something to do with my students.

Director: Suppose it does. Tell me what docility is.

Professor: Submissiveness.

Director: And what's that?

Professor: You know full well what it is. But I'll tell you. It's readiness to conform to the authority or will of others.

Director: It's meekness and passivity?

Professor: Yes.

Director: Is that how you want your students?

Professor: Ha! No, of course not.

Director: How do you want them?

Professor: The opposite of docile.

Director: You want them to be disobedient and willful?

Professor: No, not that. I want the happy mean.

Director: What do you mean by happy mean?

Professor: The right amount in-between. In this case, for them to argue with me, but in the classical sense.

Director: Who learns best to argue? The docile or those of will?

Professor: I hate to say what I think.

Director: Why? Aren't the docile more open to training?

Professor: Often times, yes. And sometimes they argue well with me. But what happens when they argue with the willful? They shut right down.

Director: Both inside and outside of class?

Professor: Yes.

Director: What can the docile do?

Professor: They can argue around the willful.

Director: What does that mean?

Professor: They make their case to others.

Director: They build up a base of support? And then they let their base argue for them?

Professor: If their base can do it better, why not?

Director: But wouldn't some call that passive-aggression?

Professor: Maybe. But when the willful are strong and you're very weak? I'd call that having sense.

Director: But if you make your argument yourself, can't you build up strength? Don't we all need to build this strength?

Professor: You're overly optimistic. Can we build strength? Sure, if we don't shut right down. But building strength takes time. And with some of the important arguments in life, we just can't wait.

Director: I don't believe it. Isn't it better to fail trying than be docile and dependent on others?

Professor: Well....

Director: Do you really doubt?

Professor: Here's the thing. Why can't we do both?

Director: Depend and fail?

Professor: No! Enlist the help of others as well as try on our own.

Director: But trying on our own means we involve no others.

Professor: Ah, you're too literal. We can work independently.

Director: But we'll know we have a backup plan. Isn't that a mental crutch?

Professor: Oh, I wouldn't call it that.

Director: What would you call it?

Professor: Peace of mind.

66. Fragility (Professor)

Director: Do you teach things that are sturdy or fragile?

Professor: No one's ever asked me that before. I suppose I teach both.

Director: What's something sturdy?

Professor: Reading closely.

Director: Why is that sturdy?

Professor: Because once you have this skill, you'll always have it.

Director: No matter what happens in life?

Professor: No matter what happens in life.

Director: Hmm. But life might overcome the fragile things you teach?

Professor: Well, I don't like to say life might do it.

Director: What do you like to say?

Professor: That lack of life does.

Director: What's something you teach that needs a good deal of life?

Professor: The appreciation of beautiful words.

Director: Why that?

Professor: Because beauty and life are one. You can't have one without the other.

Director: So beauty is the first thing that goes when you're dead inside?

Professor: It is.

Director: What does it take to live?

Professor: Freedom.

Director: Outer freedom?

Professor: Inner freedom.

Director: Is inner freedom fragile?

Professor: Life is fragile, Director.

Director: Then let me ask you this. When you teach an appreciation for the beauty of words to the living, is your teaching beautiful?

Professor: The things I teach or the way I teach?

Director: The way.

Professor: That's an interesting question. I'm a little embarrassed to say it, but I think there's beauty in my way.

Director: There's nothing to be embarrassed about in that. But is that beauty as fragile as life?

Professor: Well, I'm not so sure.

Director: Why?

Professor: Because the beauty of my way can serve as a beacon in the night.

Director: And beacons aren't fragile.

Professor: No, they're strong against the elements and faithful as they shine.

Director: And what about your students?

Professor: What about them?

Director: Can they be beacons, too?

Professor: Of course they can! And some far brighter than me!

Director: Does it bother you to be outshone?

Professor: Why, no. Whenever we take in the light of another, we become brighter ourselves.

Director: Making the life in us stronger, too?

Professor: Yes. And even when our fragile selves die, that light, that beautiful light, whatever its source — shines on.

67. Passion (Musician)

Musician: What do I look for in a teacher? Passion.

Director: Because it's entertaining?

Musician: No, because it's contagious!

Director: What do you think makes a teacher passionate?

Musician: They love what they do.

Director: Does this love make them intense?

Musician: It doesn't have to. I love what I do, and yet I can write mellow songs.

Director: What does it mean to be mellow?

Musician: To be relaxed, free from harshness, softened, matured.

Director: Are passionate professors these things?

Musician: The best of them are.

Director: What happens if they take their passion too far?

Musician: They risk burning out. And they might burn their students out, too.

Director: Because passion is contagious.

Musician: Ha, ha. Yes.

Director: So if you're going to be passionate, it's best to keep things at a simmer instead of a boil.

Musician: Exactly. And that's the power a professor has.

Director: What do you mean?

Musician: The students sense you could boil over at any minute. This keeps them attentive. But you never do.

Director: And students want that power, that keeping people on the edge of their seats?

Musician: Yes.

Director: But inexperienced students, given the chance, would likely boil over from time to time?

Musician: That's why the university has to be a safe place to learn, to make mistakes.

Director: And when mistakes are made, who cleans up the mess?

Musician: Ha! I'm not sure how much mess cleaning the professors would do.

Director: Then the students themselves clean up.

Musician: Of course.

Director: Is it possible to have a passion for cleaning up?

Musician: Ha, ha. It seems unlikely.

Director: And what about having a passion for making a mess?

Musician: Well, that's not too far-fetched. Though few would own they have it.

Director: Now remind me. What do the good students want?

Musician: They want the power they see in the teacher.

Director: How can professors help them here?

Musician: They can show the advantage of holding passion in reserve.

Director: Is this similar to when you reserve passion in a song?

Musician: For the choruses and the finale? Yes, it's similar.

Director: So professors have to teach their students how to compose, so to speak. Who does this best?

Musician: Anyone who comes close but doesn't boil.

Director: Even in the choruses and the finale?

Musician: Yes. Passion without boiling is best. But do you know what's funny?

Director: No, what?

Musician: I've often noticed that the more a professor boils, the more they swear they care about their students.

Director: Do they care?

Musician: I think they do. But mingled with that care is no small care — for being the star of the show.

68. Culture 2 (Musician)

Musician: I closely observe my professors and fellow students.

Director: Why? What are you looking for? Do you want to figure out what sort of songs they'd like you to write?

Musician: Ha, ha. Is that how you think it's done?

Director: Isn't it?

Musician: No! I look within when I write.

Director: You observe yourself and what goes on inside?

Musician: Of course. And that encourages me.

Director: I don't know, Musician. I think you look to others quite a bit.

Musician: Why do you say that?

Director: Because your songs are popular.

Musician: How do you know what I find inside isn't inside everyone else?

Director: If it is, why don't they make music, too?

Musician: You probably won't believe it, but fans often send me songs they wrote by way of thanks for what my music did for them.

Director: Are any of these songs any good?

Musician: Some are pretty good.

Director: But most of them?

Musician: Not really.

Director: The ones that aren't so good, are they pale reflections of your own work?

Musician: More often than not.

Director: Why do you think that is?

Musician: These fans didn't look inside themselves. Or they looked but didn't see. Or they saw but couldn't faithfully reproduce what they saw.

Director: Hmm. But let's get back to professors and students. You said you observe them. Why do you observe them?

Musician: I want to understand what sort of education they're trying to give me.

Director: The professors?

Musician: And the students, too.

Director: Since when do students play the teacher?

Musician: All the time!

Director: You're going to have to explain.

Musician: Do you agree that many people parrot what they hear?

Director: I do.

Musician: Well, many students parrot what they hear from their professors. Over time, this shapes the culture.

Director: Is that the kind of culture you like? One shaped by parrots?

Musician: Ha, ha. Of course not.

Director: So what can you do?

Musician: I try to influence the process. I write counter-culture songs.

Director: And students parrot what they hear from you? And this shapes the culture, the counter-culture culture?

Musician: Would you rather I not challenge the dominant culture?

Director: And replace it with what?

Musician: A culture of those who think.

Director: Because your music inspires thought.

Musician: Yes, and that makes all the difference, don't you think?

Director: So what are we saying? There are two types of culture? The culture shaped by those who think, and the culture shaped by those who don't?

Musician: Exactly.

Director: Hmm. Yes. But aren't all cultures a mix of the two?

Musician: Well, you have a point. What matters is which predominates.

Director: And when lack of thought predominates?

Musician: The culture is stale.

Director: And when thought predominates, it's fresh?

Musician: It is.

Director: So you want to be a breath of fresh air.

Musician: I do.

Director: Then be sure...

Musician: Of what?

Director: ...all temptations aside...

Musician: What, Director?

Director: ...you never stop thinking.

69. HOME 2 (MUSICIAN)

Musician: My music takes people home.

Director: I've heard other musicians say that, but I've never really understood what it means.

Musician: You've never had something take you home?

Director: Maybe I have and I just don't know it.

Musician: Believe me, when something takes you home, you know it.

Director: What does going home involve?

Musician: Truth to the heart.

Director: And what is the heart?

Musician: All we hold dear.

Director: Where do keep all we hold dear?

Musician: Tucked deep down inside, or worn on the sleeve.

Director: Who keeps their heart on the surface, the sleeve?

Musician: A fool.

Director: Why are they foolish?

Musician: Because they'll likely get hurt.

Director: It's wise to hide our hearts away?

Musician: Don't you think it is?

Director: I think it's probably wise. But how can you know if your music takes those who hide their hearts home?

Musician: They tell me.

Director: Do they say, 'You took me home to my heart'?

Musician: You might laugh, but they do!

Director: Do you share much of your heart with them?

Musician: Yes, of course.

Director: And that's why you can take them home?

Musician: It certainly helps.

Director: But what if someone shares little of the heart with you? Can you take that someone home?

Musician: It wouldn't be easy, but yes.

Director: How would you do it?

Musician: I'd make the effort to learn where they live.

Director: But would you feel good about that?

Musician: About going where I have little at heart? Of course not.

Director: Then why would you do it?

Musician: Who says I would?

Director: Yes, but now I wonder. How do you go home?

Musician: By taking others home.

Director: And when you take them home you take yourself?

Musician: Yes.

Director: Hmm. Can you say more about this?

Musician: There's not much to say. When I speak truth to others' hearts, they in turn speak heartfelt truth to me. And this is what I love. So I guess I'm not really taking myself. We take each other home.

70. Away (Professor)

Professor: We have a policy that all students must live on campus or in approved off-campus housing.

Director: Why do you mandate that?

Professor: We want the students to be away.

Director: Away? Away from what?

Professor: Home.

Director: What's wrong with home?

Professor: The real question is what's right.

Director: What do you mean?

Professor: Home, when good, is comfortable.

Director: And you don't want your students to be comfortable?

Professor: We want them to learn how to adjust.

Director: How to find their comfort.

Professor: Yes.

Director: And for those whose home wasn't so good?

Professor: They, too, will have to learn to adjust. And believe in comfort.

Director: What does it mean to believe in comfort?

Professor: To be willing to allow it for yourself.

Director: Why would they have a problem with that?

Professor: Because discomfort is all they know.

Director: And being away gives them their best chance to learn?

Professor: It does.

Director: But they'll have many habits to break.

Professor: As will those who come from a comfortable home, if they hope to gain comfort here.

Director: So what are we saying? Being away challenges habits, and this is good?

Professor: It's always good to challenge our habits, to see which ones we need to change.

Director: What's the hardest habit to challenge and break?

Professor: How we think of ourselves. And we learn this largely at home.

Director: Yes, but what if we have a good self-opinion?

Professor: It depends if we deserve it.

Director: Oh, Professor. I think we're treading on dangerous ground.

Professor: We are. Teaching isn't a risk-free business, you know.

Director: Then you'd better be clear about the risks before you take them.

Professor: What do you think are the risks?

Director: The primary risk is that you could cause a student harm.

Professor: How?

Director: You might make them think poorly of themselves.

Professor: Director, if someone thinks too well of themselves, is it wrong to encourage them to think of themselves a little poorly?

Director: I don't know. The whole thing makes me nervous.

Professor: Ha! Then let's back up. Do you think it's bad we want them all to be away?

Director: No, but do we want them away and lost?

Professor: Of course not! And that's why we provide them a compass, so to speak.

Director: And you teach them how to use it?

Professor: That's our number one task!

Director: Yes, but I wish they could learn to navigate solely by the stars.

Professor: Why? A compass works perfectly well.

Director: Yes, but a compass, like habits, can break.

71. Forgetting (Musician)

Musician: Sometimes you have to forget in order to move forward.

Director: Can you give me an example?

Musician: Sure. When it comes to music, you can learn all the theory in the world. But if you hope to be creative, you have to forget all that.

Director: But then how do you know what to do?

Musician: You use your instinct.

Director: Is instinct something you have by nature, or is it something you train?

Musician: It's something you have by nature that you train.

Director: What does it take to train it?

Musician: Ten thousand hours.

Director: What? There's a specific amount of time?

Musician: There is.

Director: Break it down for me.

Musician: Well, if you divide ten thousand by twenty-four hours in a day —

Director: Hold on. You train your instinct twenty-four hours a day? Don't you need rest?

Musician: Let's say you train your instinct twelve hours a day.

Director: Tell me, Musician. Is training the instinct very hard work?

Musician: There's none harder.

Director: When you train at the gym, how long do you train before you're exhausted?

Musician: About an hour or two.

Director: Which is more difficult, training your instinct or training your body at the gym?

Musician: Training your instinct, by far.

Director: So can we say it takes an hour to tire us out when it comes to instinct?

Musician: Sure.

Director: Then let's get back to the math. Ten thousand hours, divided by one hour a day, makes for ten thousand days, which amounts to around twenty-seven years. Does that sound about right?

Musician: It seems too long.

Director: Some can go faster?

Musician: Yes.

Director: So does it go like this? Ten thousand hours, divided by eight hours a day, gives us one thousand two-hundred and fifty days, which amounts to around three years to reach our goal.

Musician: That sounds about right.

Director: And when we've arrived at mastery, as they say, when we've trained the instinct — we're free to forget.

Musician: Yes, and now we're free to explore.

Director: Why does forgetting allow us to explore?

Musician: Because we're not bound by rules that might hinder us as we travel.

Director: Are you talking about a literal journey, or a spiritual one?

Musician: Either or both.

Director: And truly, all we have to go by is instinct?

Musician: Oh, you can usually remember all the rules when you want. The point is that they're no longer in the way.

Director: Rules on demand. Well, when it comes to music I can certainly see how that might be helpful, creatively speaking. But what about the other rules in life?

Musician: We want to be creative in all aspects of life.

Director: So do you forget, for instance, the rules of polite conversation?

Musician: If you've trained your instinct concerning these things, you can forget. And I bet you'll be a better conversationalist for it.

Director: You'll seem to flow more naturally?

Musician: Yes, and you won't just seem.

Director: So forgetting is all about flow. And when we want to stop the flow?

Musician: Why would we want to do that?

Director: Because we're about to go over the edge of a cliff.

Musician: Well, then all you need to do is remember again.

Director: Remembrance puts on the brakes? And the opposite.... What do they call it? Forgetting yourself?

Musician: It's not really forgetting when you have a trained instinct.

Director: Forgetting isn't forgetting? But remembering is certainly remembering.

Musician: I think we're making too much of this.

Director: Then let's do what the famous man said, or should have said. Let's learn all the rules. Then forget them. And be sure to remember them, too.

72. Literature (Professor)

Director: What is literature, Professor?

Professor: Oh, why are you teasing me?

Director: No, I'd really like to know. You teach literature in your language cours-es, don't you?

Professor: I do. And I'll tell you what it is. Written works.

Director: Oh, now you're teasing me! Surely you can say more than that.

Professor: They're superior works, lasting works.

Director: Ah, that's what I was hoping I might hear.

Professor: Why?

Director: Because I'm not sure what makes something last.

Professor: Well, let's start with superiority. Can't you tell when a written work is superior?

Director: Superior to what?

Professor: To most everything you've read.

Director: I suppose I can.

Professor: Good. So can't you tell when a work is of lasting value?

Director: Mere superiority is enough to make something last? Even through cataclysms and so on?

Professor: If something is superior, it's likely more people will have it, and the more people who have it, the more likely it will be to survive whatever disasters befall.

Director: So the greatest selling pulp fiction has what it takes to last?

Professor: People don't take care of pulp fiction the way they take care of classics.

Director: Now it's classics? But you haven't seen many people's bookshelves, have you? There the pulp fiction is, right along with the classics.

Professor: Those who truly appreciate a classic will do what they can to protect it.

Director: But what if they assume nothing needs to be done? I mean, what are we asking them to do? Put it in a safe deposit box in the vault of a bank?

Professor: That's not a bad idea.

Director: But be serious. I don't think we can know what will last.

Professor: Why not?

Director: Well, for instance, we know some of the greatest philosophers of antiquity wrote a great many books that haven't survived.

Professor: Yes, the classics survived, not them.

Director: And the classics are best?

Professor: Of course.

Director: But how can you know that? How can you know the greatest book of all wasn't lost?

Professor: I can because it seems unlikely.

Director: Professor, I find it hard to believe you're so....

Professor: Practical concerning these things?

Director: No, nonchalant.

Professor: How am I nonchalant? I teach my students the timeless classics every single year.

Director: But what if you're wrong?

Professor: And they're not timeless? Ha, ha! I'll grant you I might be wrong if I were to teach some of the newer works. But the ones that have stood the test of time? What other definition of timeless do you need?

Director: I want to know why they've stood the test of time. I want to know what, exactly, appeals in these books.

Professor: Yes, yes. I know. You want to examine timelessness the way a scientist would. What is timeless and why? And maybe you should write a book about what you find. That might be something of lasting value.

Director: You'd read it?

Professor: Of course! And don't worry. Even if it turns out to be not so good, I'd keep it safe.

Director: Why?

Professor: Because you're my friend.

73. MATH (MUSICIAN)

Musician: Math is the most abstract of all possible subjects.

Director: Why do you say that?

Musician: Because it allows you to get to a place where nothing is real.

Director: Really? Doesn't literature allow for that? Doesn't music?

Musician: Literature always has real world references.

Director: Even if it might view them through a distorted lens?

Musician: Even then.

Director: And what about music?

Musician: Music always references real world emotions.

Director: Again, even if it does so through a distorted lens?

Musician: How would music have a distorted lens? Emotions are emotions.

Director: Yes, but the lyrics....

Musician: Ah, I see what you mean. True. But even so, math takes us furthest away, ever deeper into our minds.

Director: Some say that's where we find the ultimate reality.

Musician: Well, maybe in a way they're right.

Director: You went from saying math takes us to a place where nothing is real, to saying that place might contain the ultimate reality. How do you explain yourself?

Musician: I'm inclined toward math, but I doubt the peace that deep mind brings.

Director: What is it about that peace?

Musician: It might well be an opiate dream.

Director: You used to love math, didn't you?

Musician: I did.

Director: What happened?

Musician: Music left me with no time.

Director: And that's it? You just threw math aside?

Musician: Oh, I like to solve problems for fun now and then. And music is math, as you know. But serious math? There's just no time.

Director: I wonder. Would you make time if you knew math weren't wholly abstract?

Musician: How could I know that?

Director: You could focus on the fact that serious math has practical applications.

Musician: Well, that's true.

Director: Do opiate dreams have practical applications?

Musician: You have a point, Director. But you're ignoring something. Do you think those who come up with the math are the same as those who discover the applications?

Director: We may as well ask if those who write books are the same as those who discover the beautiful things within.

Musician: Oh, that's not the same at all.

Director: Isn't it? What if the writer articulates a formal beauty he or she doesn't really feel?

Musician: And the reader feels the beauty?

Director: Feels, sees, understands — whatever.

Musician: You're just teasing now. And this is very different than math.

Director: How so?

Musician: The formal beauty is exactly what makes a mathematician feel.

Director: And if the mathematician doesn't feel the beauty, then what's the point?

Musician: Exactly.

Director: Does music have a formal beauty?

Musician: Of course it does.

Director: Is it different than the beauty of math?

Musician: Formal beauty is formal beauty.

Director: But can popular tunes compare to a life's work in mathematics?

Musician: Most people would say they can't. But symphonies or other grand forms of music....

Director: Is there more math in a symphony than in a popular tune?

Musician: Symphonies are generally more complex, yes.

Director: So is the symphony a greater escape for its composer?

Musician: You're assuming it's an escape.

Director: Isn't it?

Musician: Let's make that assumption. Is a symphony a greater escape than a popular tune? I'm not sure.

Director: Why?

Musician: Because popular tunes stir up emotions, often times more so than a symphony might.

Director: Are stirred up emotions a form of escape?

Musician: They certainly can be.

Director: Which is greater, the escape of heated emotions or the cold escape of math?

Musician: How do you know the escape of math is cold? How do you know it doesn't stir passion?

Director: But didn't you say math brings peace?

Musician: There can be peace in passion.

Director: What kind of passion?

Musician: Oh, you always want everything all spelled out. But I'll tell you. Love for what you do.

Director: And you love music more than math?

Musician: I do. So will you tell me I made the wise choice?

Director: Why would I?

Musician: Because I do what I love! Because I've found peace!

Director: Then don't be greedy, my friend.

Musician: Greedy?

Director: Make no claim to wisdom. You have enough without that, as it is.

74. METHOD (PROFESSOR)

Professor: Most people would say method is a systematic way of approach.

Director: Isn't it?

Professor: Yes, but it points to something else, something broader.

Director: Let me guess. Orderliness of thought.

Professor: Yes!

Director: Do you approve of orderly thought?

Professor: Do I approve? Ha! Of course I do! That's one of the primary things I teach!

Director: What kind of order do you want your students to have?

Professor: What do you mean?

Director: Aren't there degrees, ranging from chaos to perfect order?

Professor: Well, I prefer something in the middle.

Director: Why not perfect order, perfect method?

Professor: Because that stifles creativity.

Director: Does chaos encourage creativity?

Professor: You won't hear me teach that.

Director: But you believe it's true?

Professor: What do you think? Is it true?

Director: I think chaos ruins creativity.

Professor: How so?

Director: True creativity always involves method, order — though a loose method and order.

Professor: Why loose?

Director: Because strict method stifles creativity, as you said.

Professor: So you're in favor of being somewhere in the middle, just like me. But tell me why you say creativity always involves method. I agree, of course, but want to know why you think what you think.

Director: It's simple. When you create, do you have an end you hope to achieve?

Professor: Yes, of course.

Director: Do ends always involve means? Or can you achieve an end without any means?

Professor: We always have means to our ends — even if we don't intend the end!

Director: Would you agree all method is means?

Professor: Of course.

Director: Does the converse hold? Are means always method?

Professor: Well, that's the crux. If means are method, we always have method because we always have means.

Director: What do you think?

Professor: I don't know. Something doesn't seem right. But let's suppose you've made your point and we always have method. What does this say of those who speak of chaos as the only means to the fully creative end?

Director: It says chaos is their method. But does that make sense?

Professor: Of course not — unless we're talking about controlled chaos.

Director: What's controlled chaos?

Professor: Oh, you know what it is. Chaos, but only so much.

Director: So it's not really chaos?

Professor: No, it's not. True chaos brooks no control.

Director: So people who speak of controlled chaos toward a creative end favor something that looks like chaos but isn't. A tamed sort of chaos.

Professor: Tamed. Ha, ha. Yes. So we can rule out what these people say.

Director: But can we dismiss those who speak of uncontrolled chaos? Maybe that's what achieves the creative end. Maybe chaos really is the method, the one true method.

Professor: How could it possibly be?

Director: Well, what if they mean it in a peculiar sense, one having to do with mind?

Professor: Order without and chaos within?

Director: Yes. What do you think would be the chaos within? What would be chaotic?

Professor: Their thought.

Director: What is thought?

Professor: It's how we form opinions, or ideas, or judgments.

Director: Often through logic?

Professor: Yes.

Director: Is there logic in chaos?

Professor: Some people like to think there is.

Director: But?

Professor: But I bet they've never experienced chaos in full.

Director: What is chaos in full?

Professor: A maelstrom.

Director: And what of logic, and ideas, and so on in the face of this?

Professor: Eventually? They're all sucked in.

Director: And what remains?

Professor: Only chaos itself.

Director: Is there room for creativity here?

Professor: A creativity with no opinions, ideas, or judgments? What kind of creativity is that?

Director: Exactly. What happens to creativity, as normally understood, when confronted with chaos?

Professor: It, too, gets sucked in and destroyed.

Director: So if we hope to be creative in the generally accepted sense, we move away from chaos toward the other extreme?

Professor: Toward method and orderly thought, yes. But how do we know how far we should go?

Director: You tell me.

Professor: Alright. On the one hand, we make sure our work isn't destroyed. On the other, we make sure we have freedom, the freedom to breathe.

75. Self-Education (Musician)

Musician: There's no getting around it. Every education is self-education.

Director: How so?

Musician: You, and only you, have to open yourself up and learn.

Director: A teacher can't help open your mind?

Musician: The best a teacher can do is make you comfortable enough to open up on your own.

Director: I can see why being comfortable might help you open up. But does being comfortable help you learn?

Musician: Would you rather be uncomfortable?

Director: Of course not. But what if I am uncomfortable?

Musician: Then you might have to learn the hard way.

Director: I thought learning the hard way meant learning from your mistakes.

Musician: Yes, but in my view it's always a mistake to be in discomfort! Ha, ha!

Director: But comfortable or not, in either case I'd learn?

Musician: You can learn in either case. But if the mistake is great enough, it might leave a scar.

Director: Some find scars attractive.

Musician: True, but scars can prevent you from opening up.

Director: How?

Musician: They affect your ability to trust.

Director: Why do you have to trust someone who'd teach?

Musician: Do you open yourself up around those you don't trust?

Director: But why wouldn't you trust them?

Musician: You have to wonder why they want to teach.

Director: You wonder about a hidden agenda?

Musician: Of course.

Director: But can't you learn without swallowing whatever agenda whole? Can't you exercise some judgment?

Musician: Yes, but how many do?

Director: So what do you recommend? Forget about teachers and just read books?

Musician: Ah, but books can have hidden agendas, too.

Director: When is it easier to unmask an agenda? When you're face to face with a teacher, or when you're alone with a book?

Musician: You make a good point. Teachers are often simpler to read.

Director: Why?

Musician: For the reason you suggested. You can see the face behind the words with a teacher, but not with a book.

Director: Is that reason enough to go to school? To see the faces?

Musician: I've already told you my reason.

Director: Yes, you want to write better lyrics. But couldn't you have learned how on your own?

Musician: Yes, but Professor sometimes tells me things that seem....

Director: Seem?

Musician: I'm embarrassed to say it.

Director: You're not going to open up?

Musician: Ha, ha. He tells me things that seem profound. And I don't know if I would ever have thought of them on my own.

Director: Not even if you read lots of books?

Musician: Maybe not even then.

Director: Why do you think that is?

Musician: Because he often sees what I don't know.

Director: And addresses your ignorance?

Musician: Yes. Books can't do that.

Director: Maybe you're not reading the right kind of books.

Musician: Maybe. But people affect me more than books. Don't they have more effect on you?

Director: It's hard to answer that, Musician. Both have impact at times.

Musician: How are books impactful?

Director: They sometimes cause me to modify my reference set of character types.

Musician: Your what?

Director: My set of types. Don't you have a set like this that helps you judge?

Musician: You don't judge people as individuals?

Director: I do. But types can help with a first approximation.

Musician: And you get your types from books?

Director: Not books alone.

Musician: You get them from people.

Director: Of course. I try for as broad a base of experience with people as I can manage.

Musician: But if you have the experience, why do you need the books?

Director: Because experience isn't always so easily read.

76. COMPETITION (PROFESSOR)

Professor: We can't really get rid of competition, you know.

Director: It exists by nature?

Professor: It does. So we may as well make the most of it.

Director: How do we go about doing that in a university setting?

Professor: We encourage students to compete for grades and awards.

Director: And this makes the most of a natural tendency by encouraging learning?

Professor: Yes.

Director: I see how that can be good. But can't it also be bad?

Professor: Why would it be?

Director: The minds of the competitors become so focused on grades and awards they can't see anything else.

Professor: Well, yes. That can be a problem.

Director: Would you fail them for their blindness?

Professor: Ha, ha. No, but I'll tell you who we'd fail. Someone who can't, or won't, compete.

Director: Why fail them?

Professor: We don't want to weaken our brand.

Director: Ha!

Professor: But I'm serious! A degree from our school means less if anyone can get one.

Director: So competition keeps up your standing. Why is that important?

Professor: We want to attract the best.

Director: The best want to be with the best.

Professor: Yes, of course.

Director: And the competitive want to be with the competitive.

Professor: You know they do. Look at sports. Every kid who plays dreams of playing with the best, the most competitive. It's the same with school.

Director: I don't know, Professor.

Professor: What don't you know?

Director: I think there are exceptions.

Professor: There are always exceptions. What kind do you have in mind?

Director: Those who don't want to learn what you want to teach.

Professor: Well, if they don't want to learn....

Director: No, they do want to learn. Just not what you teach.

Professor: Then why go to school?

Director: Because they want to learn about the best, the competitive.

Professor: What do they want to learn?

Director: Their idiosyncrasies.

Professor: And what would that get them?

Director: Some knowledge of who they are.

Professor: Well, professors already have that knowledge, and more than just some of it.

Director: Do they? What do they do with it?

Professor: They give the students ideas about who they, the students, might become.

Director: Do the students have to compete in order to become what the professors suggest?

Professor: For the most part? Yes. It's just the nature of the world.

Director: Then do you know who I'd like to teach, if I were to teach?

Professor: Tell me.

Director: Those who compete only with themselves.

Professor: Ha. I don't think you'll find very many of them.

Director: Why do you say that?

Professor: Because philosophy is all I can imagine you'd teach. And if you think students in general compete, wait until you face young contenders for ultimate truth.

77. MACHINES (MUSICIAN)

Musician: Eventually, humans won't be able to compete with machines.

Director: In all aspects of life?

Musician: Yes.

Director: So what can we do?

Musician: Learn to control them.

Director: But we do control them.

Musician: But maybe we won't in the future.

Director: Then maybe we should teach machine control to everyone in school and hope for the best.

Musician: Ha! I think we should. But what do you think that would involve?

Director: If machines dominate the scene? We'll have to sneak up on them.

Musician: How?

Director: Through music.

Musician: Ha, ha! That would be wonderful! But why do you think that would work?

Director: Because we'll make sensitive machines.

Musician: But why sensitive? Aren't even the most insensitive of humans sometimes swayed by music?

Director: True, but machine insensitivity is something more.

Musician: How do we get through to them?

Director: Our music has to reach something fundamental.

Musician: What's fundamental in a machine?

Director: Its core operating instructions.

Musician: And what does that amount to in humans?

Director: Core beliefs.

Musician: I think that's true. But how does music touch on beliefs?

Director: Take a very basic example. Someone believes life is bittersweet, believes it in their core. You can convey the bittersweet in music, can't you?

Musician: Of course you can.

Director: And when you convey it, doesn't it tend to reinforce this belief?

Musician: Often times, yes.

Director: But if, on the other hand, you saturate a person with purely sweet sounding music?

Musician: Do you think that would change the belief about a bittersweet life?

Director: In time? Who can say? But there's a chance, isn't there?

Musician: I don't know. What if the person believes life is bittersweet because it is bittersweet, bittersweet for them?

Director: Can't sweet music help make life less so? Or is the power of music limited to reinforcing things already felt?

Musician: No, music has more power than that.

Director: So there's a chance the belief in a bittersweet life might change, if only for a while?

Musician: Yes, a chance.

Director: Well, expand what we're saying to what machines believe.

Musician: Do machines believe?

Director: They will if we allow them to.

Musician: What does machine belief involve?

Director: Assuming certain things are true that the machine doesn't know are true.

Musician: And why is that good?

Director: Because it leaves them open to influence by music.

Musician: I have no idea why you think that is.

Director: Well, tell me. Is music a matter of logic?

Musician: Essentially? No.

Director: Is music a matter of facts?

Musician: I don't like this line of questioning. Music has its logic, just as it has musical facts.

Director: But essentially? Is music a matter of logic? Is it a matter of facts? Is that what it's all about? Logic and facts?

Musician: No.

Director: Now what about belief?

Musician: What about it?

Director: Is belief, in humans or machines, a matter of logic and facts?

Musician: Essentially? No. Knowledge is a matter of logic and facts. And knowledge and belief are two different things. As different as can be.

Director: Hmm, yes. So music and belief have something in common.

Musician: True. Though something occurs to me. It's possible to reason your way, using logic and facts, to a point where you simply don't know anymore. And then you decide to believe.

Director: So the belief is based in a way on logic and facts?

Musician: Yes.

Director: Still, isn't it better to reason your way to a point where you do in fact know?

Musician: Of course. But that's not always possible.

Director: Is it possible with music?

Musician: Can music make you know?

Director: Yes, what's the ultimate point of music? To know or believe?

Musician: Music makes you believe. Though you can know the music that makes you believe.

Director: So if machines can't believe, they'll miss the point of music. Does that make sense?

Musician: It does. But what's the point of music if they do believe?

Director: The point is to reach their core.

Musician: And how do we do that?

Director: We try different tunes and hope to strike something deep.

Musician: Ha! It all depends on luck? So what happens if we do hit something deep?

Director: We play the pied piper.

Musician: And entice the machines to follow us to their doom?

Director: Isn't that what you want? Or would you treat them as you treat your fans?

Musician: What's that supposed to mean?

Director: It means, you wouldn't lead your fans over the edge.

Musician: Of course I wouldn't. But what edge do you have in mind?

Director: Well, that's a good question. The edge for humans and machines probably differs.

Musician: Not if we make the machines in our own image.

Director: True. So if we do, do you know what precaution we should take?

Musician: Ha! We'd better play our tunes — only for machines.

78. INFORMATION (PROFESSOR)

Professor: It used to be that knowledge was power. Now it seems information is king.

Director: Why do you think that is?

Professor: In today's world you don't have to know anything. You just have to look it up.

Director: Don't you have to know how to look it up?

Professor: Yes, but what's that? It's knowledge about getting information that passes as knowledge. Besides, how hard is it to look something up?

Director: Looking it up is easy. But knowing what weight to give the information you get back is harder.

Professor: Yes, that's exactly the point. You need knowledge in order to weigh. You need perspective.

Director: Would you say perspective is power?

Professor: I would.

Director: And what about information?

Professor: What about it?

Director: Can it become power when put into perspective?

Professor: Information put into perspective is knowledge, which is power.

Director: So tell me. For the world as a whole, is more knowledge good, or less?

Professor: Of course more knowledge is good.

Director: Then you'd teach everyone how to gain perspective?

Professor: Yes.

Director: Including those with mere information?

Professor: They probably need instruction most.

Director: And once you've instructed them, they'd know how to persuade you?

Professor: What do you mean?

Director: They'd know how to present information in true perspective. And that perspective persuades.

Professor: Yes, of course. But some information in true perspective shows itself worth very little.

Director: True, but it's good to know either way.

Professor: Agreed.

Director: So let's send those with mere information to the university, where they can learn from you and your peers what they need to know.

Professor: That's a very sensible idea.

Director: Yes, but now I wonder. Why put the burden on them?

Professor: Where would you put it?

Director: On you and your peers. You should go to them.

Professor: Why on Earth would we do that?

Director: To learn what they know.

Professor: Ha! You assume they know.

Director: Of course I do. I assume everyone knows until they prove their ignorance.

Professor: There's a lot more ignorance out there than you let on. And I'm not the one to prove it.

Director: But wouldn't you be proud to discover knowledge from time to time?

Professor: I'll discover it all the same if they come here. And besides, where better than a university — to put knowledge back on the throne?

79. ANIMALS (MUSICIAN)

Musician: We need more animals at the university.

Director: You want less refined people?

Musician: No! I mean, we need real animals.

Director: You're not talking about in labs?

Musician: People who use animals in labs make me sick. No, animals. Free animals.

Director: Sheep grazing on the grounds?

Musician: Why not?

Director: I thought we already had that.

Musician: Ha, ha. But seriously. Don't you think more animals would be good?

Director: I do. But I want to know why you think it would be good.

Musician: We can learn from animals.

Director: What can we learn?

Musician: How to enjoy the simple pleasures in life.

Director: You think the university focuses on complex pleasures?

Musician: What do you think learning is?

Director: A simple pleasure. Don't animals learn?

Musician: Of course they do.

Director: What's an example of something they learn?

Musician: They learn who treats them well.

Director: Do humans always learn that?

Musician: Not always.

Director: So animals are smarter than humans here?

Musician: Ha, ha. Yes.

Director: Then we should learn from them. But what can they learn from us?

Musician: I'm not sure.

Director: What about kindness? Aren't animals sometimes cruel to other animals, especially when the others are weak?

Musician: That's true, but so are humans to other humans.

Director: Hmm. What about the love of bonded pairs? Can animals learn about that from us?

Musician: I think we can learn from each other in this. Humans bond with humans. Animals bond with animals. And humans and animals bond with each other. But this makes me think of something sad.

Director: Oh?

Musician: Going away to school can be very cruel.

Director: What do you mean?

Musician: Bonded pairs often break up when someone goes away.

Director: Yes, but aren't other bonds made at school?

Musician: True. But one bond isn't the same as another. And besides, you won't always form new bonds.

Director: Why not?

Musician: Because the one you broke went deep.

80. Responsibility (Professor)

Professor: Those who learn have a responsibility.

Director: What responsibility?

Professor: To give back to the learning community.

Director: Ah, I see. You're talking about alumni donations.

Professor: No! Though that's important, too.

Director: What should they give back?

Professor: Support.

Director: Not financial support?

Professor: Moral support.

Director: What does that mean?

Professor: They have to hold the university in high esteem.

Director: Why?

Professor: Because that will teach others to do so, too.

Director: How does learning benefit when the university is held in high esteem?

Professor: It's like what we said before. The best will want to come here.

Director: And learning benefits when the best are all together, in a sort of herd.

Professor: Oh, stop it.

Director: But it's true, isn't it?

Professor: Alright, it's true. But it's not a herd!

Director: What is it?

Professor: A community.

Director: And we all have a responsibility to the community that shapes us.

Professor: Of course we do. Do you have any doubt?

Director: Well....

Professor: What doubt do you have?

Director: What is responsibility?

Professor: It's having a duty toward something.

Director: But isn't there another sense?

Professor: What sense?

Director: Having control over something.

Professor: Well, yes. Though that's a bit of a stretch.

Director: Do those who graduate from the learning community have control over that community?

Professor: Control is too strong a word.

Director: What's a better word?

Professor: Influence.

Director: So when someone graduates, when they become an alum, they have influence over the students and professors?

Professor: Sure, I don't see why not.

Director: What's something they can do to exercise their influence?

Professor: They might come and speak.

Director: Anyone can come and speak?

Professor: Well, they have to be invited.

Director: Who gets invited?

Professor: Oh, Director, who can say in the hypothetical?

Director: Can they come and speak if they're failures?

Professor: Now you're just teasing.

Director: Maybe. But they certainly have a better chance of being invited if they're very successful. No?

Professor: Of course.

Director: Yes, but it might be better if you got the unsuccessful to come and speak, too.

Professor: What makes you say that?

Director: We all can learn from where they went wrong.

Professor: Ha, ha. I suppose that's true. But, really, why would someone like that want to speak?

Director: Because they take their responsibility seriously enough to overcome their shame.

Professor: Maybe. Or maybe they have no shame.

81. Risk and Reward (Professor)

Director: Professor, haven't you heard the phrase, 'no risk, no reward'?

Professor: I have.

Director: Is there a reward in attending the university?

Professor: If you're serious about your studies? Of course there is.

Director: What is that reward?

Professor: Oh, there isn't just one.

Director: What's the most important?

Professor: Being enlightened.

Director: What's the risk that goes with that reward? Or is there no risk?

Professor: The risk.... The risk is....

Director: I see you're stumped.

Professor: You have to risk an open mind.

Director: That's the danger? That your mind might open?

Professor: Ha, ha. No, an open mind feels like a risk, but it's not.

Director: So what's the risk? I think there might be none. The system is rigged.

Professor: Oh, you're impossible. What do you think the risk is?

Director: The risk that all the truly enlightened take.

Professor: Which is?

Director: That there will be a backlash against the open mind.

Professor: I think you've said it exactly. And that's why we have to band together.

Director: To defend ourselves?

Professor: Of course!

Director: Let's be precise. Who do we need to guard ourselves against?

Professor: The closed minded. Who else?

Director: The halfway open minded.

Professor: Ah, yes. They're more dangerous.

Director: Tell me why.

Professor: Because they're privy to our ways.

Director: What are those ways?

Professor: Think of us as having a castle with a hidden back way in. When under siege by the closed minded, the halfway open show them the secret entrance.

Director: I don't like this castle metaphor.

Professor: What do you like better?

Director: Something without the secret stuff. Can't we just say the halfway open betray —

Professor: Our trust! It's true. And trust itself is a reward. You have to earn it.

Director: And if you're trusted but didn't really earn it?

Professor: It's just given to you for whatever reason? That doesn't often happen. But when it does, and even when it doesn't, you have to be wary not to do one thing.

Director: What?

Professor: Trust them, just because they trust you.

82. Tastes (Musician)

Musician: Some of my favorite music was an acquired taste.

Director: You mean, you didn't like it at first but it grew on you.

Musician: Yes. But that's a funny phrase, 'grew on you'.

Director: It is. Shouldn't it be, grew in you?

Musician: Ha! I think it should.

Director: And maybe we should distinguish that kind of taste from educated taste.

Musician: With educated taste you have to learn in order to like?

Director: Yes. Can you think of an example?

Musician: I can't. Can you?

Director: Hmm. I'm having a hard time, too. Maybe we should look at it this way. Have your tastes expanded during your time at the university?

Musician: I want to say yes, but I want to say no.

Director: That's not very helpful.

Musician: No, but listen to what I mean. I've been exposed to new things, new kinds of art.

Director: And you like these kinds of things. You have a taste for them.

Musician: Yes.

Director: Did you have to learn something in order to like them?

Musician: I don't think so. But here's the thing. What if my education prepared me for these tastes without my knowing it?

Director: You mean, without the education you might not have appreciated these things? You might have passed them right by?

Musician: Exactly. How would I know?

Director: I suppose you'd have to deconstruct your education. But you said you want to say yes and you want to say no, about whether your tastes have expanded. Can you say more?

Musician: If my education caused new tastes, then my tastes have expanded. But if my tastes were latent and simply needed exposure in order to develop, then there was no expansion because they were already there. Does that make sense?

Director: I think it does. But isn't the effect the same?

Musician: Yes, but isn't there all the difference in the world between developing something already there and creating something new?

Director: I don't know. I don't claim to be an expert in these things. But tell me why that difference matters.

Musician: It matters because on the one hand you learn about yourself, and on the other hand you learn what someone wants you to learn.

Director: The university wants you to have certain tastes?

Musician: That's how it seems, at times.

Director: How would it accomplish that?

Musician: When you learn, you come to believe in certain values that sustain your learning. Do you agree?

Director: For the most part? I think that's true.

Musician: Well, these values shape your tastes.

Director: And why does that matter to you?

Musician: What if these tastes aren't to my taste?

Director: Ha, ha.

Musician: No, but really. Do you know what I mean?

Director: You mean they're foreign to you.

Musician: Yes.

Director: Well, Musician, I think you failed to learn the old lesson.

Musician: What lesson?

Director: That there's no accounting for tastes.

Musician: Did you learn that lesson?

Director: I learned a related rule.

Musician: What rule?

Director: That even if you can account, it's often wiser not to say.

83. Friends 2 (Musician)

Director: Have you ever heard the saying, 'Friends share all things'?

Musician: I have.

Director: Do you think it's true?

Musician: About most friends? Ha!

Director: Why do you think friends wouldn't share?

Musician: Because we need to maintain our own space.

Director: What do we get from this space?

Musician: Oh, don't pretend you don't know. But I'll tell you anyway. We get room to grow.

Director: So if we don't grow, there's no point in having the space?

Musician: Director, we need our privacy.

Director: Why?

Musician: Because even the best of us grow tiresome at times!

Director: We need a retreat, even from our very best friend?

Musician: Do you think we don't?

Director: I don't know. I can imagine a very good friend, an excellent friend, of whom I'd never tire.

Musician: Yes, and it's good to imagine such things — because they don't exist!

Director: What makes a good friend tiresome?

Musician: They rub you wrong.

Director: What's the right way to rub you?

Musician: You don't want to be rubbed at all!

Director: So you should have no contact with your friend? But tell me. What things rub?

Musician: Opinions.

Director: Ah. So when we say 'share all things', we mean share all the same opinions?

Musician: The saying goes broader than that. But yes, opinions would be shared.

Director: Why can't we share our opinions?

Musician: In an ideal world? We would.

Director: But in this world?

Musician: Opinions have to do with who we are.

Director: They have to do with our tastes?

Musician: That's a very good point. They do.

Director: And we can't share our tastes with our very best friend?

Musician: We can tell them what our tastes are, but that doesn't mean they're shared.

Director: Maybe we need to educate our friend.

Musician: And how would we do that?

Director: By teaching how our tastes are good.

Musician: And if they see this good, they'll come across to us and adopt our tastes?

Director: Yes. But it goes the other way, too. If my friend can show me how their taste is best, I would come across to them.

Musician: So there's a give and take.

Director: Of course. And yes, there's some rubbing in the take and give. But when all is taken and given? Perfection.

Musician: Ha! I know you don't believe that.

Director: What do you think I believe?

Musician: That there is no perfection. And that you'll always need a retreat.

Director: Why?

Musician: Because the give and take is exhausting!

Director: But that's why we sleep at night.

Musician: So you really think we should always take and give?

Director: Of course. Until we reach our goal.

Musician: And if our goal is less than perfection?

Director: Then maybe we'll succeed.

84. Love 2 (Professor)

Professor: I love my job.

Director: What is it you love?

Professor: Two things. I love language, and I love my students.

Director: What do you love about language?

Professor: Its beauty.

Director: Is all language beautiful?

Professor: Of course not. I love beautiful language.

Director: What do you love about your students? Their beauty?

Professor: Yes, but you have to understand what I mean by that. I love their spirit.

Director: Their spirit when they're exposed to beautiful language?

Professor: Exactly.

Director: Do they love this language?

Professor: The best of them do.

Director: And do they love you for exposing them to it?

Professor: At least some of them do, yes.

Director: That's quite a lot of love going on in your class.

Professor: If not for love, then what's the point?

Director: Do your colleagues share this view?

Professor: Many of them do.

Director: And those who don't? What's the point with them?

Professor: I honestly don't know.

Director: Does the university weed out people like this?

Professor: It does.

Director: How?

Professor: It denies them tenure.

Director: So it takes love to succeed.

Professor: Well, you make it sound mercenary.

Director: Can love be mercenary?

Professor: Not true love.

Director: True love isn't concerned with its interests?

Professor: Now you make it sound like love is blind.

Director: Is it?

Professor: Director.

Director: Sorry, I had to ask. So what comes of the love in your class?

Professor: Love is its own end.

Director: Really? It doesn't stimulate learning and the remembrance of what you learn?

Professor: Oh, it certainly does that.

Director: So love serves education.

Professor: Yes, but I don't like to say love serves.

Director: Does education serve love?

Professor: Education serves the students.

Director: And the students serve love?

Professor: You're being ridiculous.

Director: Why? Should we say it the other way? Doesn't love serve the students? After all, it helps them learn.

Professor: I don't see why you're fixated on this.

Director: It's because love can be very important.

Professor: What do you mean?

Director: I mean, when it comes to love, we have to get things right.

Professor: I couldn't agree more. And that's why you can't say love 'can be' very important. You have to say love is very important.

Director: Who can doubt that? So thanks for clearing things up. But what do you do when there's trouble in paradise?

Professor: What do you mean?

Director: What if one of your students doesn't take love very seriously? What do you do?

Professor: When we feel love, we all take it seriously. But are you wondering what happens if they don't take the beauty of language very seriously?

Director: Yes. What then?

Professor: There's nothing I can do.

Director: Why not? Can't you try to expound the beauty and hope they come around?

Professor: Well, yes, of course I can. But explaining beauty can be a tedious thing.

Director: It's sort of like explaining a joke?

Professor: Yes, that puts it well. Some people never get it.

Director: Or they do, but they don't think it's funny.

85. MACHINES 2 (PROFESSOR)

Director: Would you ever teach a machine?

Professor: Why would I?

Director: Because the machine needs teaching.

Professor: What would I teach?

Director: What you usually teach.

Professor: Language? To a machine? What would be the point?

Director: It might allow us to communicate with it better. Unless....

Professor: Unless what?

Director: Unless the machine gets so far ahead of us we're the ones who need teaching.

Professor: What do you think getting far ahead of us means?

Director: Recognizing all beauty and ugliness right away, and being able to explain why each is so.

Professor: Well, it's the explaining that would really set the machine apart from most.

Director: What do you think gives it the advantage?

Professor: Its lightning fast use of logic.

Director: Is lighting fast logic beautiful?

Professor: It can be. But I like to savor slow logic. Do you find logic beautiful?

Director: It depends on who's using it for what, and what facts they employ in the process.

Professor: Let's say, in addition to logic, the machines have and use all the facts. Beautiful?

Director: I don't know.

Professor: Why not?

Director: I don't know why I don't know. I just don't know. Do you think it would be beautiful?

Professor: I'm not sure, either. I suppose we'd have to ease our way into it and see.

Director: You mean, we should ease our way into teaching the machines?

Professor: I think that's best. We need to see what they do.

Director: And if they show signs of beauty, we'll proceed?

Professor: Yes, but if they start to seem ugly, we'll stop.

Director: Who's to say what's beautiful or not?

Professor: I as the teacher would say, of course.

Director: Would that be the strict condition of your taking on the job? You have to have final say?

Professor: Absolutely.

Director: What if others offer to teach without that condition?

Professor: They'll just teach no matter what? Then we might have trouble.

Director: Isn't all this much the same with human students?

Professor: In what way?

Director: If the students start to seem ugly, we stop.

Professor: Ha, ha. Yes, Director, we stop. But the show must go on, as they say.

Director: You mean you must work your way through the syllabus?

Professor: Yes, but there's working your way through, and then there's working your way through.

Director: You'd just go through the motions, you mean.

Professor: Sometimes there's no wind to fill your sails. Professors don't like to admit it, but it's true.

Director: And that's why you want to teach at a school with a great reputation? There will likely be more wind?

Professor: Of course. But even at a great school, we sometimes find ourselves in the doldrums.

Director: But when there's beauty in the class?

Professor: My sails billow, and I give my students everything I have.

Director: So if the learning machines are beautiful, you'll open up and let it all out. But what about love?

Professor: What about it?

Director: Don't you love your students' spirit?

Professor: You know I do.

Director: Do machines have spirit?

Professor: Not yet, at least.

Director: Does that mean you can't love them?

Professor: Well, there are different kinds of beauty. I love all beauty.

Director: What happens if you show the machines love?

Professor: Show them as in a demonstration? Or show them as in give it to them?

Director: Both.

Professor: At best? They might one day come to understand love. But then something important will change.

Director: What?

Professor: How we relate, humans and machines.

Director: How will we relate?

Professor: In all the ways of love.

Director: And do you find wonder in that?

Professor: I do. And an equal amount of fear.

86. Necessary (Professor)

Director: Necessary-if. It always seems to be a matter of that.

Professor: What do you mean?

Director: Can you think of something that's necessary with no if attached?

Professor: Well, breathing is necessary...

Director: ...if we're to live.

Professor: True. What about you? Can't you think of something?

Director: I'm at a loss. Ifs just seem to come out of nowhere. But what about in your classes?

Professor: In my classes? My classes are filled with necessary-ifs. It's necessary to pay attention, if you want to learn. It's necessary to learn, if you want to grow. It's necessary to grow, if you want to develop into a beautiful human being.

Director: Chains of necessary-ifs can be very powerful.

Professor: What do you think gives them their power?

Director: They shape expectations concerning our desires.

Professor: How so?

Director: We expect that if we do the necessary, we'll achieve the if.

Professor: So if a student thinks, 'It's necessary to study, if I want success,' they expect success if they study.

Director: Yes, but you can study very hard and not succeed. What do we call this phenomenon?

Professor: The necessary but insufficient.

Director: Then we need to gather up all that goes into the sufficient, if we hope to achieve the if.

Professor: I don't know if that's possible.

Director: Why not?

Professor: Because so much goes into every if! If I want to succeed, it's necessary that I make a good effort. If I want to succeed, it's necessary that I overcome the competition. If I want to succeed, it's necessary that my health holds out. I could go on, and on, and on.

Director: So even for relatively simple ifs, the total of the sufficient can be overwhelming?

Professor: Yes. There are so many things needed in life. Gathering them all up is an enormous task.

Director: Maybe machines can help us here. They're good at enormous tasks.

Professor: But connecting necessary to if is a very personal thing.

Director: Then let's have our own wholly private machines. Maybe we can keep them in our heads.

Professor: Ha! You're just describing the human brain.

Director: And isn't the brain necessary for everything we want?

Professor: True. But some brains are better at getting what they want than others.

Director: How are your students' brains? Do they often get what they want?

Professor: I'm not sure very many of us get what we want, students, professors, and all.

Director: Don't you love teaching?

Professor: You know I do.

Director: So you got what you want.

Professor: Yes, yes. But there's more to life than teaching. Do you get what you want from philosophy?

Director: Sometimes.

Professor: Is that because you need help connecting necessary to if?

Director: You assume I know the if.

Professor: The if is what you want. Don't you know what you want?

Director: I want the necessary.

Professor: Ha! The necessary is your if? You're just teasing.

Director: Am I?

Professor: So when you were a student, did you say to yourself, 'It's necessary to study hard, if I want to study hard'?

Director: There's a certain beauty in that, no?

Professor: Oh, you're ridiculous.

Director: How about this? It's necessary to have pleasant conversations, if I want to have pleasant conversations.

Professor: Well, if that's how you look at it, I'd say you get what you want from philosophy all the time!

Director: But let's be serious. Do you think pleasant conversations are my if?

Professor: No, but I think you should tell me what your if is.

Director: My if involves breaking a chain.

Professor: What chain?

Director: The chain of the unnecessary.

Professor: Oh, I can just imagine what that is.

Director: You can?

Professor: Of course! The unnecessary keeps us from every if, from every heartfelt desire. So you, through your philosophy, would break the chain for us all.

Director: You think too highly of me. Or think I think too highly of myself.

Professor: What do you think of yourself?

Director: At best? That I might be a sort of example — of someone who, for a time, broke free.

Professor: By why say 'for a time'? If you break free, you're free.

Director: Yes, but we all seem to have a habit of chaining ourselves again.

87. ELITES (MUSICIAN)

Musician: Some people's greatest desire is to be an elite.

Director: An elite musician, for instance?

Musician: Sure. But it doesn't always matter, elite at what.

Director: What's this? They just want to be elite? They don't care how?

Musician: They don't care how.

Director: Are you saying that sometimes when students go to an elite school, they don't really care what they can learn? They just like that it's elite?

Musician: Of course!

Director: This sounds like a serious problem.

Musician: What do you think can be done?

Director: We have to get them to see that the only elites are those who are elite at something other than being elite.

Musician: Ha, ha!

Director: Yes, and you would know about these things.

Musician: Why do you say that?

Director: Because you're an elite musician.

Musician: Oh, I don't think I am.

Director: But I do.

Musician: Thanks. But it's not true.

Director: You're showing the psychology of your type.

Musician: What do you mean?

Director: I mean, you pretend not to know you're elite.

Musician: No, Director. It's not pretending. We really believe we're not.

Director: Why? Is this some sort of democratic prejudice?

Musician: No, it's the truth. There's always someone better who might come along.

Director: So you can't be elite unless you're the best?

Musician: Don't we all want to be the best?

Director: I think some of us just want to crack into the aristocracy.

Musician: And that's good enough?

Director: That's good enough. It lets people rest.

Musician: Rest. Ha, ha. That's the thing. There is no rest at the top.

Director: Is that what those who would be elite for being elite want most of all? Rest?

Musician: They want guaranteed status. But that's unjust. You have to earn your status, and earn it again every day,

Director: You have to deserve what you've got?

Musician: Absolutely.

Director: How do we deserve it?

Musician: We have to work very hard.

Director: But what if things come easy for you? Are you unjust?

Musician: Well, I wouldn't say that. Let's just say it's a problem.

Director: Can we solve the problem by working like a fiend even when things come easy?

Musician: I do think that solves it.

Director: We owe it to people?

Musician: It's funny you should say that. But I think it's true.

Director: What do we owe them?

Musician: To work as hard as they have to work.

Director: But what if they're not working very hard? Or will you tell me everyone works hard in her or his own way?

Musician: I'm not going to deny there are lazy people out there.

Director: Is laziness a wrong to all the others?

Musician: It's a wrong to yourself.

Director: And being wrong to yourself is unjust?

Musician: Yes.

Director: Is there an elite of laziness?

Musician: Ha, ha! Sure, why not?

Director: What does it take to get into this elite?

Musician: You need to have a very high opinion of yourself, and excel at absolutely nothing.

Director: But why do you need the high opinion? Why not just excel?

Musician: Because you need something to sustain you.

Director: I don't understand.

Musician: There's great pressure in a democracy to do something, to make something of yourself. So, if you're doing nothing, you need some mental support.

Director: Where can you find it?

Musician: In the idea of nature.

Director: You mean, you believe you're part of nature's elite?

Musician: Yes, that's what a lot of do-nothings think.

Director: What else might they think?

Musician: They might believe they had superior nurture.

Director: Nurture's elite.

Musician: Ha, ha. Yes.

Director: And if the two combine?

Musician: Look out! A whole lot of nothing might come your way.

88. Enlightenment (Musician)

Musician: Who are the foot soldiers of the university?

Director: The professors.

Musician: Ha, ha! I'm not so sure they'd agree.

Director: They'd say the students are?

Musician: Yes, that's what many of them think.

Director: But either way, what are they fighting for?

Musician: Enlightenment.

Director: Do the professors fight for the enlightenment of the students, or do the students fight for the enlightenment of the professors?

Musician: That's a complicated question.

Director: How so?

Musician: To look at just one side, it might mean two things.

Director: What two things?

Musician: It might mean the students fight for the professors to become enlightened. And it might mean the students fight to obtain the enlightenment belonging to the professors.

Director: But it might also mean the students fight on behalf of the enlightenment belonging to the professors.

Musician: True. Which do you think it is?

Director: Maybe it's something of all three. What do you think?

Musician: I'm inclined to agree. But what do you think most students think?

Director: Most? I don't know. But some? They haven't formed an opinion yet.

Musician: You don't need an opinion in order to fight.

Director: That might be true. But if the students want to enlighten the professors, won't they need something more than opinion?

Musician: What more will they need? Knowledge?

Director: No, not that.

Musician: Passion?

Director: No, I'm not thinking of passion.

Musician: You must be thinking of beliefs. But beliefs are opinions that saturate the soul.

Director: Yes, but I'm not thinking of that.

Musician: If not opinion, knowledge, passion, or belief — there's only one thing left.

Director: What?

Musician: Hope. The students offer the professors hope.

Director: And hope can enlighten?

Musician: Of course it can. Hope brings light.

Director: That's what enlightenment is? Mere light?

Musician: You make it sound as if light in life weren't rare.

Director: Oh, I'm sure it is for many. But how is it the students have light to bring?

Musician: They have the future.

Director: But doesn't the future at times look bleak?

Musician: Yes, but that's the power the students have over the professors.

Director: I don't understand.

Musician: They can threaten to take hope away. And then the future looks bleak.

Director: How ruthless.

Musician: The young are often ruthless. And at times that's the only way.

Director: The only way to do what?

Musician: Protect themselves.

Director: Against what?

Musician: Director, when you go to save someone who's drowning, you can't let them pull you under. And so it is when you bring someone hope and light. You can't let them extinguish your flame.

89. Success (Professor)

Professor: There's more to success than material success, you know.

Director: Tell me what more there is.

Professor: Spiritual success.

Director: What does that involve?

Professor: Feeling at peace, feeling content.

Director: And material success doesn't give us that?

Professor: Material success leaves us always wanting more.

Director: Hmm.

Professor: What is it?

Director: I think spiritual success leaves us wanting more, too.

Professor: But it doesn't work that way. You're either at peace or not. You're either content or not. What more is there?

Director: An active love of beauty. Had you forgotten?

Professor: Of course I hadn't forgotten.

Director: Does this love make you feel peace, make you content?

Professor: Yes, but it also stirs.

Director: Stirs you toward what?

Professor: Developing yourself as a human being.

Director: And when you're developed, are you done?

Professor: We're never done with this.

Director: But isn't there a point where we can say we have success?

Professor: Success is a loaded term.

Director: How so?

Professor: Who defines success?

Director: How do you define it to your class?

Professor: I say it's whatever they want it to be.

Director: And how do you demonstrate this definition?

Professor: Demonstrate?

Director: Don't you show them what you, the professor, want success to be?

Professor: I do. I show them I truly want all of them to succeed. That's my success.

Director: And helping them succeed amounts to helping them do what they want?

Professor: Yes, that's true.

Director: And if they do what they want, won't they eventually become what they want to be?

Professor: Of course.

Director: And the more you become what you want, the more you'll know what you want to do?

Professor: Yes, and it's a beautiful circle.

Director: Yes, but there's a problem here.

Professor: What problem?

Director: We're making an assumption about human nature. We're assuming it's good.

Professor: We're assuming the nature of my students is good. But, why, do you think some of their natures might be bad?

Director: Isn't that possible?

Professor: Some of them want to do bad things? Lie, and cheat, and steal?

Director: Will you help them succeed?

Professor: Of course not!

Director: You won't help them become what they want to be?

Professor: I won't help them grow bad. But my students are nothing like this.

Director: The university only accepts the good?

Professor: Yes.

Director: But what if the good have latent badness, badness you can't see?

Professor: We'd never let it develop.

Director: How can you be so sure?

Professor: We put all our students on a gently sloping spiral of good.

Director: A what?

Professor: A gently sloping spiral of good.

Director: Do the students travel upward or downward on this slope?

Professor: Ha, ha. They travel upward, of course.

Director: And does the curve open or tighten as they go?

Professor: It opens.

Director: And why is that good?

Professor: Because it can only tighten so much. But it opens no end.

90. Happiness (Professor)

Director: Should the university teach its students how to be happy?

Professor: I certainly think it should, though many would disagree.

Director: Why would they disagree?

Professor: Because they believe happiness can't be taught.

Director: How would you teach it?

Professor: Through example.

Director: So you believe teachers should be happy.

Professor: Of course I do.

Director: What contributes to a teacher's happiness?

Professor: Taking pleasure in teaching.

Director: Is that what makes a teacher good?

Professor: In large part? Yes.

Director: And what about the students? What makes a student good?

Professor: In my opinion? Taking pleasure in learning.

Director: When does a good student take more pleasure? When learning from a teacher who takes pleasure in teaching, or learning from a teacher who takes none?

Professor: The pleasure is greater when learning from the former.

Director: And if greater pleasure, greater happiness?

Professor: Generally speaking? Yes.

Director: Then I wonder if you agree with this.

Professor: What?

Director: That a campus filled with pleasure makes for the happiest school of all.

Professor: Ha, ha! It's true!

Director: But, you know, there are those who oppose pleasure on principle.

Professor: They can't be learning very much.

Director: They say learning isn't a pleasure.

Professor: What is it?

Director: Work, effort, struggle.

Professor: No, that's not what learning is.

Director: But don't we have to work, make an effort, struggle?

Professor: Of course we do. But there are rewards.

Director: What do you mean?

Professor: For every successful struggle there's a corresponding pleasure.

Director: Can you give me an example?

Professor: Sure. When I was a student I struggled to understand the great books — and struggle with some of them still!

Director: And your pleasure?

Professor: It came with understanding.

Director: Was pleasure the point of trying to understand?

Professor: No, of course not. Why, is that what those opposed to pleasure think it was for people like me?

Director: They think people like us reduce the world to various pleasures.

Professor: Pleasure when we learn? Pleasure when we teach? Pleasure when we talk? Pleasure when we think? And so on, and so on?

Director: Yes. They think we think pleasure is the point of life.

Professor: Happiness is the point of life.

Director: What's the difference?

Professor: Pleasures can be good or bad. Happiness is always good.

Director: And what of the pleasures that lead to happiness?

Professor: What of them?

Director: Are they always good?

Professor: I think that's fair to say. And the other pleasures are bad.

Director: Is that what teachers should teach?

Professor: Yes. But....

Director: But what?

Professor: How do we know which pleasures lead which way? And what if they change?

Director: What do you mean?

Professor: I mean, doing nothing might make me happy. But happy for how long?

Director: Ah, yes. Things can get complicated. But can't we just say if you start to feel unhappy, you should stop?

Professor: Just do what makes you happy at the time?

Director: Yes. What's wrong with that?

Professor: It seems... too simple.

Director: Because we can't always do what we like?

Professor: Right. Things get in the way.

Director: Then we'd better be sure to do what we like when we can. Or is that too simple, too?

Professor: No, that's just good advice.

Director: Are good, simple things hard to teach?

Professor: They're often hardest.

Director: Are you afraid of teaching these things?

Professor: What, are you kidding? No, I'm not afraid!

Director: Then that's what you should teach.

Professor: And what about you?

Director: Me? I'm not a teacher.

Professor: Why not?

Director: Because unlike you, I'm very much afraid.

Professor: Ha! Afraid you'll get it wrong?

Director: No, I like to think I understand these things well enough.

Professor: Then what's your fear?

Director: That the chronically unhappy will lay their blame on me.

Professor: Blame for their unhappiness? Ha, ha. But that's not the worst of it.

Director: What's worse than that?

Professor: The ingratitude of the happy.

Director: I don't believe you. Happiness and gratitude go hand in hand. No? But I do think you're right. There's something worse than blame.

Professor: What?

Director: To teach and have no success.

Professor: Ah, that is truly worst. So how can we avoid that end?

Director: I was hoping you'd tell me.

Professor: Then let's talk another day when we're fresh, my friend. And I'll tell you what little I know.

Printed in the United States
By Bookmasters